SRI LANKA DIARIES

A Couple's Travel Journal

With 75 Tips to Help Plan Your Trip

SARAH CARIGNAN & CEDRIC LOISELLE

DEDICATION

To the kind Sri Lankans who left us with fond and lasting memories.

CONTENTS

PREFACE

This is a travelling couple's journal of a 19-day holiday in Sri Lanka. Every day, the first entry is told from Cedric's point of view because, firstly, it was his idea to write this book and because he is more succinct. The second entry is my (Sarah's) take on the day.

DAY 1: DECEMBER 18, 2014

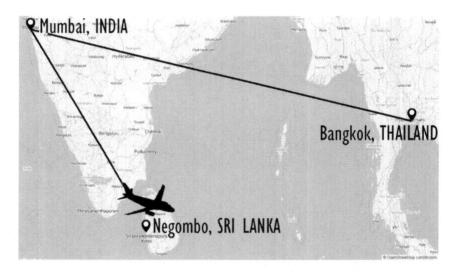

We arrive at Sri Lanka's Bandaranaike International Airport after a long travel day. Yesterday we traveled by bus to Bangkok from Hua Hin, where we have been living for 4 months. We stayed at the Aranta Hotel near Bangkok's airport. This morning we took a 6 am flight to Mumbai, hung out for 6 hours at Mumbai's airport, then boarded our connecting flight to Sri Lanka's international airport in Negombo, which is about 40 minutes' drive to the capital city of Colombo.

By the way, Mumbai's airport is by far the nicest airport I have seen in my life. During our 6-hour layover there, we tried an India restaurant and it was absolutely delicious. We had paneer, chicken, roti, naan and more, and it was a delight. Definitely some of the best Indian food I've had in my life.

Negombo's airport, on the other hand, is the ugliest airport I've seen in my life. Right when you set foot in the airport, you can tell that you are about to visit a poor country. Much poorer than any other I've seen (granted, I haven't seen that many). The airport is simply very old, in disrepair, looks like it was built in the '70s, and barely maintained. (Postscript fact check: it was actually built in 1967.)

Upon arrival, we knew we needed to do two things at the airport: get a free SIM card from the leading 3G provider and withdraw money at the ATM to take a cab to our hotel. I read online that you pick up the free SIM card at the immigration counter. While being processed into the country at the immigration counter, I ask, "Do you have free SIM card?"

The agent stares at me with mild disapproval. Pursing her lips together so that the corners of her mouth downturn, she slowly shakes, "SIM card finish."

Being in Asia for the past 4 months, I know to just accept this answer and not ask any questions. I move past immigration, turn a couple corners, descend escalators, and voilà! I see a lonely Dialog (name of cell phone company) counter with a bearded man sitting there. I go and get my free SIM card. Nice! One thing done. We keep walking and find an ATM, great! We withdraw money, no problem.

TIP 1 – This is a cash country. If you prefer to bring cash (vs. using Sri Lankan ATM), bring USD or EUR. You will get a better rate than your home currency and it will be more easily exchanged.

Next we go to the taxi counter. I tell the lady behind the counter where we want to go and show her the address. She tells me it's going to be 970 Sri Lankan Rupees (around $10) and that I pay the taxi driver at the end.

Our taxi is an old minivan with no seatbelt, but we get to the hotel without issue. The taxi driver had to call the host for directions as he neared the destination because he couldn't find it. They always call, this is very typical in the Asian countries I've visited. The addresses are not accurate, or hard to find, or they don't have an address at all. During the ride I notice many, many things; there are a lot of: pedestrians, bicycles, buses, very old cars, and very, very old things. Not much new at all. In fact, it's like I have been transported back to the 1970s.

TIP 2 – Make sure you have your guesthouse phone number for your taxi driver. Unless you are staying in a major hotel (and even then), chances are he will need to call them for directions.

When we arrive, the taxi driver tells me, "1,970 rupees."

I say, "No, it's 970 rupees." He grabs the receipt and shows it to me. It indeed says 1,970 rupees on the receipt. Not much I can do now. I pay 2,000 rupees in vain. I just took one of the most expensive taxi ride of my life, in the poorest country I have ever visited. It just cost me around $20 for a 15-minute taxi ride. I had read online that it should cost around 700 rupees. In comparison, a similar ride from the Bangkok airport (Thailand, a much richer country) would cost around 140 Thai Baht (around $4 USD). In Canada (where taxis are prohibitively expensive), a similar ride would probably cost $20-25. I feel like I just got robbed.

At the guesthouse, Villa Taprobane, we are warmly received by the owners. The guesthouse is basically a large home with 4 bedrooms. They show us to our room. My first impression of the room is kind of bad. But just from the ride to this guesthouse, I recognise how poor this country is, and I have to lower my standards. The bed is alright, with a very thin sheet provided. The provided towels are extremely old and stained and the communal bar of soap is old with plenty of curly hairs on them.

TIP 3 – If you will be staying in 2 -3 stars guesthouses, bring soap as most of them don't provide any (or they will provide used bars of soap if any). Bring bar soap if the plane won't let you travel with liquid.

In situations like these, you can either cry or laugh; we sleep. I am dead tired and sleep like a rock. Oh and by the way, it's raining.

DAY 1: SARAH'S TAKE

Our flight to Sri Lanka has one stop, a 6-hour layover in Mumbai. The cheapest direct flight from Bangkok to Sri Lanka only takes about 3.5 hours and cost $800 CAD (Round Trip for 2 people). However, this price is brought to you by Malaysian Airlines. The year 2014 put Malaysian Airlines on the map; they were newsworthy in March after their plane left Kuala Lumpur and disappeared without a trace in the Indian Ocean and again in July when another plane was shot down over Ukraine. They say there's no such thing as bad publicity. I disagree.

The second cheapest direct flight nears $1,200 (RT for 2 people). We chose a flight with Jet Airways that only costs $400 (RT for 2), but takes all day (6 am to 9 pm). Jet Airways was a small, economy airline in India that recently branched out into "full service flying" and offered incredible promotional prices in September when we booked this Christmas trip to Sri Lanka.

We are at Bangkok's Suvarnabhumi (pronounced "Sue-wanna-poom") airport and a sign at our gate indicates all flights to India must go through "an additional security screening" before boarding. The additional security screening is a lot like a concert or festival bag check. The first security agent is annoyed and distracted. It's that attitude of a high-level employee with a lot on her plate, replacing a lower level employee who didn't show up for work. She seems like she has much better things to be doing while she unzips my carry-on and she feels around inside the bag.

This trip we are backpacking it with carry-ons only, so our bags fit the maximum dimensions exactly. Despite my bag being quite stuffed, the security agent doesn't take anything out or even look inside. I wonder what she is rummaging around for that she only needs her hand to identify it. After passing this bag check, I step onto a platform where a very bored employee does a wand body scan. I am wearing a belt with a large metallic buckle and this doesn't set off the wand, but my left knee (no zips or buttons there) make the machine beep like crazy. She clears me without further investigating my knee.

Cedric and I reflect on the extra security measures and wonder what they accomplish compared to the normal security check of a full body scan, X-ray baggage, etc. Anytime there is extra security, I dwell on unknown dangers and get a little paranoid. We start observing the other passengers with suspicion as we wait to board our plane.

After a dreadful flight (toddler seated behind), we arrive in Mumbai. Before

7

we can leave, an announcement informs us, "Indian law mandates all international flights must be sprayed with an insecticide. This spray is deemed safe by the WHO, but may irritate some people." The flight attendants walk briskly down the aisle spraying what looks like an aerosol bathroom freshener. I see many Indian passengers covering their face with their sleeve to protect against the spray. Given India's lackluster hygiene standards, we figure that if they are protecting themselves, we *definitely* need to cover our mouth. At first, it smells like peach, then after a couple of minutes the smell becomes heavy and cloying. Since the flight crew didn't open the overhead luggage compartments, I wonder how many bugs the spray is really killing. So far, the extra security measures of the Indian government leave me puzzled.

Before we can enter Mumbai's airport terminal and wait for our next plane, we must pass through a security check for international transfers. With rich carpeting, brass stanchions holding velvet ropes, soothing music, and a long counter, it gives a hotel lobby vibe. With no sign, passengers milling about everywhere and a group of staff just chatting together behind the counter, we are confused about what to do here. We have 6 hours to kill, so we just hang back and hope it will become clear with time. The passenger in front of us, an older gentleman, guides us to the correct area and we wait for an agent at the counter to break away from her chat and help us. Handing over our boarding pass and passport, the woman tells us firmly, "No. I don't want to see your passport."

We only had to show our passport back in Thailand to Thai security agents. It seems odd that with so many additional security measures, India doesn't require the basic one. After our boarding passes are stamped, she gives us bright yellow tags with no explanation. We are holding onto the tags and looking lost. Again, the kind gentleman in front of us explains that we need to put the tags onto every bag. He shakes his head and shrugs apologetically, "This country is nonsense..." This does not seem like his first trip to India.

We arrive at the security screening area and there are two lines: one long and one short. Cedric and I join the short line. There is a big commotion with unintelligible yelling. A passenger kindly explains that I need to join the women's line. Just like women's washrooms, the line is three times longer and slower than the men's. After passing the walk-through metal detector, whether you made it beep or not, a security agent goes over you again with a handheld metal detector. Men have this all done in the open. Women go into a small, curtained booth where a female agent passes the wand.

Ladies' bags are brought through the X-ray scanner while we are still waiting our turn to have the double metal detection. Our bags travel along the conveyor, get X-rayed and wait out of sight at the end of the security area. Many women gesture and shout to their men (who already passed security) to take their belongings. I see my man about 30-feet away, sitting on a bench, nose in his smartphone, and oblivious to the commotion. I catch a glimpse of my abandoned purse and bag. The male security staff have their backs to the cleared items. Instead, they are turned staring at us, the women, and laughing with each other. Not one of them is paying any attention to the bags lingering at the end of the conveyor, which contain passports, cell phones, wallets, laptops, etc.

We take an escalator up to the main terminal. It is all polished marble, glass and brass. Very clean, luxurious and reminds me of an upscale shopping mall. There are plenty of comfortable seats, charging stations with cables for many types of mobile devices, computers (need local SIM card to login) and desks where you can charge and work on your own laptop.

We arrive at noon and had excitedly planned on eating at Subway. Subway in India makes local subs like: paneer tikka, aloo patty, chicken tandoori, etc. To our great disappointment, Subway is not in our terminal and the food court is quite small. Every stall is barren, except "Street Foods by Punjab Grill," which has about 200 people in a line snaking around the food court. I turn to Cedric and say, "We've got to eat there." But we decide to wait a while, until there are fewer people in line.

Every time I enter a bathroom in this airport, I am accompanied by a female washroom attendant and shown to a stall, like I'm being shown to a table at a restaurant. One time, I enter a bathroom with no attendant and a male crew is fixing something in the very back of the washroom. I head to a free stall, but the female attendant stops me. Instead, she leads me out of the washroom, down the hall to a large private bathroom with changing station and wheelchair access. Just like the extra security measures in Bangkok, this makes me feel the opposite of safe; I feel nervous and paranoid.

The Mumbai airport is full of 20-something, Indian men headed to Dubai. There are hourly flights to this UAE city, importing cheap labour to build their desert oasis. There are no other white couples in the airport, so we get our fair share of glances from these young men. We are also gawk-worthy in Thailand, but Thais make an effort to hide it and always look away when we make eye contact. When Cedric leaves for 20 minutes to track down the airport's Wi-Fi password, the vultures circle. It is not long before the empty hallway fills up with young men. No one talks or approaches me, they just glare, unsmiling and unwavering. I haven't seen a security guard for a while and feel more uncomfortable with every passing minute.

Time is dragging by and Cedric has been gone for what seems like hours. I reflect on the recent news reports about rape and violence against women in India. To be in a luxury airport terminal and feel uneasy...I certainly wouldn't want to travel solo. Even a "safe country" like the United States is number 1 in the world for yearly reported rapes. When Cedric returns to my side, the vultures scatter and the staring goes back to a comfortable level. We charge our devices and do some work at the work stations.

At around 2 pm when Punjab Grill is deserted, we split a Paneer makhani (butter chicken sauce). We like to start by splitting one meal because most restaurant portions are too big for one person. It comes with whole wheat roti, pickle (onion slaw), rolled papad and spicy dal fry. It's so unbelievably delicious. A near-religious food experience at the airport cafeteria. Cedric goes back for a second plate; chicken makhani this time. Even better than the paneer because of the chicken tikka (chunks of chicken marinated in yogurt and spices then cooked in a tandoor). This time we take it with freshly baked naan bread. Oh my…

TIP 4 – Bring USD, EUR or credit card to pay for food etc. in your layover airport.

As we board the plane to Sri Lanka, a security guard checks that all bags have the bright yellow tag given to us upon arrival. One passenger has a fancy-looking bottle of alcohol without the appropriate tags and is pulled aside. He is desperately trying to reason with security not to take it away as we enter the plane.

Our Jet Airways flight to Sri Lanka has a fun and frantic energy. Lots of families with small children fill the air with chatter. There are snacks, free drinks (including alcohol and full cans of beer), a full meal, and tea served on this 2-hour flight! The flight crew is so polite ("Here is your second beer") and accommodating ("Yes, let me move the snack cart all the way back so you can go to the washroom") that they are still serving food when the pilot announces we are descending into Sri Lanka.

As with most flights, we are not given arrival cards on the plane. We must hunt for them once landed because there are no signs indicating their location. They are near the Immigration counter, but of course, there is no pen at the arrival card station.

TIP 5 – Bring a pen in your carry on to fill out your arrival card on the plane or in the airport where either there will be no pen or 10 people will be waiting to use it.

We bought our Sri Lankan tourist visa online a week prior to leaving. It was surprisingly high-tech and easy, and it gave me a nice first impression of Sri Lanka. There weren't any instructions to print anything, but I printed the email confirmation just in case.

The visa must go into their system because at Immigration, I only had to show my passport and arrival card, and I was allowed in the country. After the Immigration counter and before customs, we pass about 100 small shops selling TVs, fridges, cell phones, etc. I love a good deal, but it's too loud, too bright and disorienting (like a casino) to make sound decisions (like a casino).

TIP 6 – Unless you are from Singapore, Seychelles or the Maldives (you don't need a visa if you are from one of these countries), buy your visa online (http://www.eta.gov.lk/slvisa/) prior to arriving. It's a bit cheaper than getting a visa on arrival, the process is very easy and efficient and it will be one less thing to worry about when arriving in Sri Lanka.

No one is working customs, so we just walk through to the arrivals area. There are several booths doing currency exchanges, but no ATMs in sight. Behind the wall of currency exchange booths is a large TV facing rows of chairs. Most of the chairs are occupied with people staring zombie-like at the TV screen. There are a lot of chairs and I wonder what so many people are doing here at 10 at night. We walk all around before spotting the lonely ATM hidden on the far side of the furthest bank booth. Cedric tries his debit card and it works.

TIP 7 – If you will be using a debit card for ATM withdrawals, make sure it's got the Cirrus, Plus or Maestro logo on the back. But as you will find out later in this book, even if your card and the ATM machine have one of the corresponding major logos, the transaction might still fail, especially in small towns. For this reason, bring a zero balance credit card exclusively for ATM cash advances, just in case your debit card doesn't work. Don't forget to bring your online banking info to pay it back right away. However, even credit cards might still not work either in smaller towns. You best bet is to withdraw money in one of the two major cities in the country, namely Colombo (metropolitan) and Kandy. If you need to withdraw money at the airport, there are a couple of ATMs near the exit, not too far from the taxi counters. They worked for us.

With our free SIM card in hand, we head over the Dialog counter, a company with the best cell plans. It is on the far wall, behind all the TV zombies. Cedric sees an ad for a good plan (700 international minutes, 200 local minutes, 3 GB data for 1299 rupees or $10). Cedric tells the agent we have the tourist SIM card and wants the advertised plan. The agent asks, "Have you activated your SIM card, sir?"

"Not yet, we just arrived."

The agent says, "Ah. Well, sir it takes 2 hours to activate the SIM card and I can't give you that plan until the card is activated."

Cedric and I look at each other, we don't want to wait 2 hours. Then the agent reassures us, "If you don't want to wait 2 hours, I can activate your card now and give you this plan." He points to an ad on his counter, it is more expensive with less options. We are tempted to go for it, just to have it done, but while we are reading the ad, the agent serves another customer. It's just long enough that we lose the sense of urgency and leave, deciding to deal with the cell plan later.

TIP 8 – Make sure to bring an unlocked phone, get your free SIM card from Dialog at the airport and just follow the instructions to activate it, it's actually very easy. Once the SIM card is activated, you need to buy a plan. Get the tourist plan. To buy it (if the guy at the Dialog counter in the airport doesn't want to do it), you can go to any shop in the city with the big Dialog logo. We went to a shop near the Colombo Fort train station, it was very easy and they were very helpful. Also, Sri Lanka has a different GSM cellular frequency than North America. Make sure your cell phone can handle the 900/1800 bands.

We are right near the exit, we hesitate about whether we should go outside and find a taxi or try to look for a service in the airport. In our experience, you get a better rate dealing with the airport's taxi service than going out on the street and haggling for yourself. I spot a counter with "Airport Taxi" near the currency booths. We show the turquoise-saried employee the address of where we want to go and she says it costs 970 rupees. She is very soft spoken, so we get her to repeat it several times. Cedric asks one last time, "It is 970 rupees?"

She nods.

TIP 9 – Get the taxi to write down the price if there is the slightest hint of miscommunication.

She takes about 10 minutes typing away on a keyboard hidden behind the tall counter. I admire her sari during this time. Finally, we hear the high-pitched buzz of a dot matrix printer. Summoned by the noise, a portly gentleman strides toward the counter, beaming at us. He grabs the feed paper. Glancing at it, he says, "This is a wonderful hotel, you will like it."

The guesthouse only has a couple rooms and is quite far from the airport, so I am shocked that he would comment on it. I ask him, "You know it?"

He just smiles and ignores me. He leads us out of the airport at a brisk pace. Not far from the exit is a dense crowd of people waiting behind a rope, holding name signs. Men, women and children are here to greet their newly arrived parties. We approach two boys laughing and playing on our side of the rope. Behind them, an employee steers a huge line of luggage carts back into the airport. Our guide stops and yells viciously at the boys for about a minute. As we walk away, the kids slowly return to the crowd, looking very ashamed.

Outside, it's hot, dark and raining. I am sweating in my plane outfit of jeans and a sweater. There are decorative lights everywhere and it looks very festive. My first winter without snow, I keep forgetting it is Christmastime.

TIP 10 – Change out of your warm plane clothes before leaving the airport. Many taxis have no air conditioning.

A row of old minivans lines the long, covered sidewalk. A group of taxi drivers are chatting when our guide bursts into the circle, speaking to them authoritatively in, presumably, Sinhalese. They take a look at the paper in his hand and for the next 5 minutes, they all discuss and gesture in various directions. Trying to be helpful, Cedric shows them the mapped directions on his smartphone. They glance at it, but strangely this doesn't resolve anything. (How can a perfectly plotted course not clarify how to get there?) They keep discussing.

Eventually, our guide points to one of the men and says, "OK, he will drive you. Goodbye." After he leaves, there is another 5-minute chat among the taxi drivers; hand gestures indicate they are still trying to figure out where to take us. Our assigned taxi driver walks us to his minivan a ways down the long sidewalk and chats with a couple of other drivers about the address. At his taxi van, he finally breaks down and calls our guesthouse for directions, then we are on our way.

The minivan is old and the seatbelts don't work. It smells like a garage—gasoline, motor oil and dust. The driver honks every time he passes someone (pedestrian, bicycle, motorbike, tuk tuk, car, bus.) Lights and flowers beautifully decorate the main street outside the airport. As we travel along a large boulevard, it looks like any other small city; I see many shops and billboards announcing brands I don't recognize. I spot a KFC and feel some familiarity. We turn off the main road and there are much fewer street lamps. There are a lot of mostly short, skinny pedestrians. I see five men walking down the street, wearing a sarong tied at the waist and a long-sleeve, button-down shirt, each balancing a large, overstuffed armchair on their head. I have never seen people move furniture 1.5 times their size like this.

The taxi driver stops a cyclist in the middle of a railroad crossing and I assume he is asking for directions. I find it unbelievable that our driver has chosen to place himself directly on the train tracks to absorb himself in a conversation. It's even a bit rude to involve the man on the bicycle, who would have a much slower getaway. Although I tell myself it would be improbable for a train to come at that moment, I am planning our escape (Unlock the door, grab the handle, pull sliding door, grab bags...). After a minute of their chatting, the unlikely happens; I see a train light approaching. I can hardly believe it. My pulse starts to race as my adrenaline rush hits. Luckily, the driver sees the light too. He finishes his conversation and slowly drives off the tracks, reaching for his cell phone to call the guesthouse again. He makes the call off the tracks. It's an old cell. The kind that came out after the old flip phone. I remember a Motorola just like it back in 2001.

We arrive at our destination and our host is smiling with an umbrella at the gate. Cedric gives the taxi driver a 1,000 rupee note and there is an awkward exchange, as it becomes clear we misunderstood the mumbling woman at the taxi counter and the total trip cost 1,970 rupees. (Post script note: we later learn from the guesthouse owner that a fair price would have been 700 rupees.)

TIP 11 – Contact your host beforehand to determine the reasonable taxi fare from the airport to their accommodation.

The guesthouse is a large two-storey home, with a huge yard and a towering Christmas tree set up in the spacious living room. We are shown to our room. We booked a "Double Room with Private External Bathroom Air Conditioning." There's no air conditioning, the bathroom is shared, and everything is kind of grubby with whitish walls that haven't been washed in years, but the room is big and there is a standing fan.

I am exhausted and try to sleep. But Cedric gets the Wi-Fi password and is messing about with our tech: charging things (this house has an adapter we can use), checking tomorrow's travel plan online, and setting up the SIM card. By the way, the SIM card only takes 2 minutes to activate and not the "2 hours, sir" as quoted by the airport's Dialog agent.

I hear noises in the kitchen and hope they are not preparing anything for us. Yes, they are. The host knocks on our door to offer us some tea. Though I would have loved some, it's too late for caffeine and part of me is unsure whether we'll be charged for it, so I decline. He looks crestfallen and I feel bad.

TIP 12 – Most guesthouses will offer complimentary tea when you arrive and it's rather impolite to refuse it.

I head to the shared bathroom for a shower. The toilet, bidet and sink are all a matching set of maroon-coloured ceramic. They say they have hot water, but the shower has several cut-outs at the top and on the sides to a yard. Not sure whose yard or how much they can see into the shower, so I decide to wait until our next hotel.

An hour later, Cedric is finally ready to sleep and we set up the mosquito net over the bed. Within minutes, Cedric's rhythmic breathing tells me he is asleep. I lie awake for several hours, annoyed that after an exhausting day of travel, my window for sleep seems to have passed.

DAY 2: DECEMBER 19, 2014

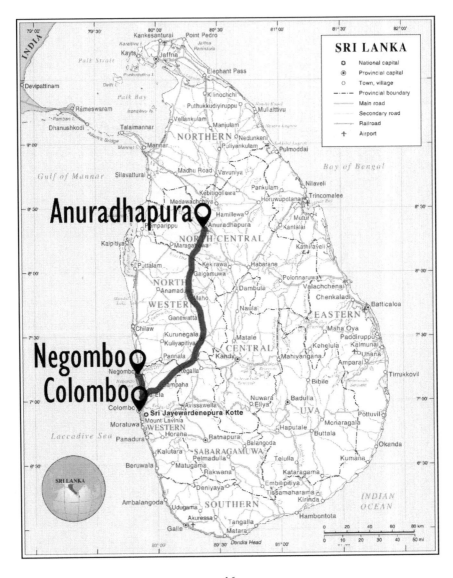

We get up at around 8 am, as we have yet another long travel day ahead of us. Today we want to either take the train or bus to Anuradhapura, a long way from Negombo (4 to 6 hours by bus or train, respectively). Soon after getting up, the owner knocks on our door to tell us that breakfast is served. Great! I had forgotten that breakfast was included! I made the hotel reservations several months ago, so I couldn't remember what was included.

We sit at the table with two other guests, one French and one Japanese. We are served omelette, sausages and fresh fruit. It is delicious. The owners are preparing and serving the food themselves. As we eat breakfast, it doesn't take long before all of us start bombarding the owners with questions about how to travel to our next destinations. The owners are extremely helpful and knowledgeable and answer every question that every single one of us have.

Upon receiving information from the owners, we decide to take the train because we think this will guarantee us a seat. To take the train, we first need to take a commuter train from Negombo to Colombo. Then from Colombo we take a train to Anuradhapura. The owners call us a taxi and we go to the local train station to take the commuter train. The taxi ride costs us 200 rupees.

We arrive at the local train station, I cannot believe what I am seeing. The train station is basically the same station that was built when the British were here 70 years ago, along with the furniture and everything. I feel like I am on a movie set. No, I feel like I just travelled back in time. No, I feel like I am in a real-life Fort Edmonton, the largest living history museum in Canada. I don't know exactly what I feel, but it is definitely surreal. We buy our tickets, 45 rupees (around $0.45) each, and wait. The train arrives and we embark. Not surprisingly, the wagons are similar to the station. They look like 70-year-old wagons, probably because they are.

I sit beside a gentleman and he starts talking to me, asking me where I am from and if I like Sri Lanka so far, to which I say, "Yes, of course." Wouldn't want to disappoint a proud countryman. Not that I don't like Sri Lanka so far but, to say the least, it simply…I am actually not sure which adjective to use, let's just say, it is fascinating. Unfortunately, the conversation is cut short because I don't understand half of what the man is saying. His English is very broken and as a non-native English speaker, it's hard for me to understand him.

As we get closer and closer to Colombo, the train really fills up. It is a commuter train used by workers, trying to make it in the big city. Most people are relatively well-dressed, but there are also a lot of people who seem very poor. So far, another thing that I've noticed is that the overwhelming majority of people have a very basic cell phone (one that you can buy for $30 in Canada). It is striking because in Thailand everyone has a smartphone. Samsung mainly, but also Apple and other Thai brands. This is another indicator of how poor this country is.

On the road, there are lots and lots of buses, pedestrians and bicycles. Seems like buses are the main mode of transportation. By contrast, in Thailand (except Bangkok, where there is a great public transportation system) most everyone has their own motorbike (scooter). There are few pedestrians and most bicycles you see have a white person on them, usually cycling for sport. Nobody walks anywhere. (I make a comparison with

Thailand, simply because it is an Asian country and I live there.)

Once in Colombo, we need to buy our ticket to Anuradhapura. When we enter the ticket office, we are not sure if we're going to get tickets; they have signs everywhere that say all trains are full until the end of December. We go wait in line anyways and hope for the best. We wait maybe 10 minutes. An old man comes up beside us and cuts in front when it is our turn. Then we wait another 5 minutes and ask the agent for good news. Thankfully, they do have tickets! We buy them at 450 rupees each and feel relief. The train leaves at 4 o'clock and we want to buy a power adapter and cell plan for our new SIM card. So we make it a mission to do these things in the free time that we have.

We exit the train station and there are literally thousands of small shops selling everything under the sun. It looks very hopeful. After 1 hour of shopping around, we are able to find a power adapter and activate our SIM card. By the way, so far we find that most people are very kind and very helpful. If you need anything, you just ask around and people are all very happy to help you. And they almost all speak English. Quite good English too, far better than in Thailand.

TIP 13 – Kind Sri Lankan exception: most tuk tuk drivers will bend the truth in their favour. If you need to ask them something, make sure you corroborate their information with other people.

We now have Internet on our smartphone and it feels great. So, I look for a good restaurant. We are exhausted and hot after shopping around with our heavy backpacks for the past hour. We find a restaurant, go eat, chill, and we are ready for the train ride.

We have 2nd class tickets, so our seats are reserved. But the people in 3rd class don't get a reserved seat; it's first come first served. If you don't get a seat then you do the whole journey standing up. So as the train arrives there is a wave of people pushing to jump on before it stops. The pushing and shoving reminds me of Black Friday/Boxing Day back home. We walk to our wagon, away from the war in 3rd class wagons. It's actually not bad at all. The seats are relatively comfortable and leg room is good. The train leaves and we are finally en route to our first real destination: Anuradhapura.

TIP 14 – Forget about saving a couple bucks with the train's 3rd class, get your reserved 1st or 2nd class seats if they are available. Also, determine if your travel dates include Sri Lankan school or national holidays. If so, more locals will be filling up trains and buses throughout the country. Things may be fully booked and packed with people. In that case, definitely book your train tickets in advance

through an agent online.

The train ride is absolutely mental. Sarah took her motion sickness pills and thank God she did because this would have been a puke fest. It bounces left, right, up, down, like a roller coaster. There are no washrooms aboard the train. We knew this, so we purposefully didn't drink much 2-3 hours before our train ride. It works; I don't have to pee for the whole trip. I witness a father helping his 4-year-old daughter to pee in the corridor between train cars. The train stops a couple of time, but as the announcements are in Sinhalese, we only realize these are bathroom breaks after we leave the train.

We arrive in Anuradhapura and a man approaches us, asking us where we are going, saying he has a good hotel for us. We ignore him, as I read there are a lot of these touts and they can be persistent. I try to ignore him as much as possible in the hope he will give up, but he doesn't. He walks with us and keeps asking us where we are going and telling us he has good hotel. I give in and tell him I have a reservation. He asks me which hotel. I continue ignoring him. He persists. I reply again that I already have a reservation to which he replies, "I'm only transportation."

We keep walking and I ask him, "You have a taxi?"

He says "Yes, this one." I pull out my phone and show him our hotel name. He says he knows it and knows exactly where it is. I ask how much and he says, "100 rupees" (around $1). That is actually a very reasonable amount. I say ok and we get in his tuk tuk. On the way there he asks us where we are from, he whistles and kind of dances. Very funny. (Postscript note: He was actually our nicest and most reasonably priced driver of the whole trip in Sri Lanka.)

We get to the hotel and, once again, receive a warm welcome from the hotel staff. They show us to our room and spray the mosquitoes in the room. Very kind reception. The room is actually a lot better than our previous one. The soap provided is, once again, old bars of soap. This time I break down and use it. Got to lower my standards. I wash the soap and then I wash myself. The towel provided is very old, thin, stained. Got to lower my standards, no choice. I just use it anyways. Reminds me of when I was a kid, the whole family shared 1 bar of soap and our towels were old, thin, and stained. Reminds me of Chef Ramsay when he yells, "Standards!" to his crew in Hell's Kitchen (wanting them to elevate their standards). But in my case, I need to lower them.

We go to bed. I am extremely tired, this was another very, very long travel day. I sleep like a rock. Oh and by the way, it's raining.

DAY 2: SARAH'S TAKE

I wake up in Villa Taprobane feeling terrible. I didn't sleep much last night and am still exhausted, but I just want to leave this place and move onto the next, hoping for better. I hear dishes and know they are preparing breakfast for us. I don't have high hopes for this meal and hope we can duck out before it is served. Cedric is still packing up when our hosts tell us breakfast is ready. I am hiding out in the bathroom, dawdling, wondering how I can avoid this meal without seeming rude.

Eventually, I head to the dining area and am blown away by the sight. A round table covered with a white table cloth and full place settings; this is miles above the grubbiness of our room and the bathroom. In the light of day, the house is also a lot nicer than I realized. With a waterfall in a sitting room off the large kitchen-living room area, I think these folks must be quite wealthy. Their yard is very large, green and lush with tall, stately trees.

Cedric and two other guests are seated at the table. Our hosts are a husband and wife. The wife is cooking in a kitchen out of sight and the husband is delivering food to the table. Each guest is served, on lovely plateware: an omelette with sautéed onions (heavily salted, but delicious), two little spicy sausages, a plate of fruit (papaya, pineapple, apple), a mountain of toast, butter and jam. Our host serves us a champagne flute of fresh coconut water and asks if we want coffee or tea. We receive our own tea/coffee pot with cup, saucer, spoon, milk and sugar pot. This is 5-star service.

It is very silent at the table until the husband asks me where we are from. This melts some of the tension and gets everyone talking. We meet the other guests, a 40-something Japanese woman and 50-something French man. The Japanese woman is eating a Sri Lankan breakfast of string hoppers and a couple of curries with her fingers. The wife host proudly says she also asked for the Sri Lanka meal last night. This Japanese woman is throwing herself into the Sri Lankan experience and I appreciate her gusto, wondering if I should be doing the same.

We timidly ask the host a couple questions about the bus station and soon everyone at the table is confirming logistics of upcoming travels ("How do I go…How much for…How long does it take?") The hosts are very patient and thorough in answering our questions. They give us advice that you can only get from a local ("If you get off at this station, you will get a seat when you transfer trains…If you take that bus, you might not get a seat.") An hour passes in a flash and I regret my earlier dawdling, wishing we had more time to spend with this interesting group of people.

TIP 15 – Ask your host plenty of questions. Input with a local perspective is invaluable.

Our host asks how we will get to Anuradhapura, our next destination about 176 km north. We say maybe the train, maybe the bus. He recommends we take the bus as it is only a 4-hour ride and because we are at the start of the line, we would get seats. He warns us that the train departs only from the capital of Colombo. We would need to take a 2-hour ride to Colombo on a 3rd class commuter train and take another 6-hour train to reach our destination. Cedric mentions to our host that the Sri Lanka Railway website shows a 4-hour express train to our destination. Our host shakes his head slightly and smiles, "No, it is 6 hours." I know that smile. It is a knowing smile, an "oh, those silly tourists" smile, the "you'll see" smile.

Cedric insists about the express train and shows our host the webpage, our host shrugs and agrees that the website does indeed say 4 hours. Though I hope for a 4-hour train ride as advertised, I trust our host and know it will be longer. But we need to buy train tickets for later in our trip and I read we could buy them in Colombo. When I ask our host if we can buy tickets at our next destination, he shrugs and says, "Maybe." Not a convincing answer.

Since I have so much motion sickness, Cedric wants me to decide on the mode of transportation. I choose the train mainly because that way we go to Colombo and we can buy all the train tickets for the rest of our trip.

We get ready to walk to the train station, but our host says that since they are re-tarring the road, we will probably ruin our shoes if we walk. He tells us that normally he would drive us, but he is already offered to drive the Frenchman. He calls us a tuk tuk and we head over to the train station. Wouldn't you know? It's exactly where our driver stopped to last night.

The station is a blast from the past. It's dark inside, either there is no electricity or they don't turn it on. We buy our tickets from a grumpy old guy sitting in a little room on the other side of a small barred window. We head out to wait on the platform with everyone else. A decrepit wagon sits on the far tracks and doesn't inspire much confidence.

I see quite a few people walking on a worn dirt path between the tracks. As good as a sidewalk, I guess, but I can't help thinking about all the signs and announcements in North American train stations about staying off the track. I've heard so many commercials and news reports about people dying on the train tracks that I'm under the impression they are incredibly dangerous. So far, Sri Lankans are showing me there's nothing to be afraid of. When the train approaches, I understand why. Seemingly, our average speed is 20 km/h.

Although I took a Dramamine pill for this 35 km trip, I still keep my eyes closed for the 2-hour train ride into Sri Lanka's capital city. I know motion sickness hits people differently. Some people have it worse if they can't see, but for me it's a lifesaver. (Albeit annoying that I miss most things.) When the train stops at each station, I open my eyes to see more people embarking and food sellers popping on to wander the aisles with baskets of snacks, chanting what they have on offer. A man, his two legs wasting and disfigured, hobbles around on crutches also chanting. Sometimes these criers hop off before the train crawls away from the station, sometimes they stay on and leave at the next stop.

Cedric is sitting beside me and I hear, rather than see, that he has been sucked into a conversation with an elderly gentleman. The man asks where we come from and what we think of Sri Lanka. Cedric has trouble understanding, asking him to repeat often. I understand the old guy, but am too hazy from my Dramamine to be of any assistance. Eventually Cedric admits English is not his first language, that he is French. The old man responds by bursting out a stream of rudimentary Italian, "Buongiorno, arrivederci, uno, due, tre…" which makes me giggle.

After a suitable amount of time has passed, the man asks Cedric for money. He does it in such a subtle way, with extensive preamble and proud justification, that Cedric doesn't follow. He gets the old man to repeat again and again saying, "I'm sorry, I don't understand." The old man finally gives up and the conversation ends.

Cedric isn't an actor, meaning he doesn't manipulate and can't lie effectively. So, I recognize that he is not pretending and that he really doesn't understand the old guy. But his conversation makes me realize that speaking French and playing dumb could be a useful way for us to avoid some uncomfortable situations. Then it dawns on me that we've repeatedly been victim to people "not understanding" our English to their benefit.

The Colombo train station is a gong show. Jam packed with people moving every which way and we have no idea how to get out. I chase after some people from our train before they disappear from sight and they eventually lead us to the exit. We wander outside the station until we see a booth that reads "Reservations." When we enter and there is a huge chalkboard listing routes and dates—at the end of each line it says "FULL." There are 6 booths, each with a different destination on a sign above the window. All of the booths showing our destinations have a little sign "SOLD OUT UNTIL DEC 30" taped up.

TIP 16 – The train is a must and seats can sell out quickly. When we travelled, Sri Lanka Railways train tickets could be reserved 45 days in advance, but not online. You must be in Sri Lanka to buy these tickets. You can book online with private train carriages (ExpoRail, Rajadhani) or contact your hotel/local travel agencies to secure them

on your behalf. Consider the most scenic side of the train carriage (west side if travelling Galle to Colombo for ocean view) and select these seats.

Only 1st and 2nd class seats can be reserved, 3rd class is first come first serve and mainly standing room only. We get tickets for today's trip, but before we can figure out which line to stand in for the rest of our tickets, we are quickly ushered out of the room. Of course, they are closing for lunch.

TIP 17 – Take into account that the train's reservation offices close for lunch between noon and 1 pm.

Across the street from the train station is a long alley bustling with people and overflowing shops. There is a chain-link fence on the road, so that we can't cross to the other side. I watch where the crowd is walking and spot a pedestrian overpass. We walk around asking where to buy a prepaid cell plan and power converter.

TIP 18 – There are 2 types of power outlets that are equally used. To plug in your electronics, get the universal adapter or just buy both adapter types because they only cost a couple dollars in Sri Lanka (compared to $30 at the Mumbai airport).

Our guard is up. Before we left, we read about scammers and are very suspicious of what people say. But our experience couldn't be better. People on the street were helpful, the power converter was cheap and the cell agent gave us excellent salesmanship and service. We left that street feeling better about Sri Lanka.

TIP 19 – After the cell phone store sets up your cell plan, make sure you try calling/browsing the web before you leave the store. They may have to do additional tweaking on your foreign phone.

After seeing no sit-down restaurants around the train station, Cedric spots an American chain on Google Maps: TGI Friday's. It is another low 30°C day with our big bags and by the time we reach the restaurant, we are incredibly sweaty and tired. The air conditioning is blasting inside this American-themed restaurant. We both order the veggie burger and the patty (deep-fried mashed potato with green peas and onion) is about 6 inches in diameter. It is served with a large portion of fries and there must be a total of 4 potatoes on the plate. We remind ourselves to always start with one portion and split it! We try to pay by MasterCard, but the transaction is declined.

TIP 20 – Some stores and restaurants that accept credit cards may actually block foreign cards, so be sure to have some cash on hand.

Returning to the train station chilled and full, we walk toward the reservation area to buy tickets for the rest of our trip. A gentleman approaches Cedric and says with full authority, "You need tickets, sir. Follow me." Obviously the guy is BS and I think we should just go to the reservation office that we were at before, but Cedric follows the guy, and I follow Cedric. We enter an office that looks nothing like the rest of the train station and he tells us, "Sit, the agent is on his way." We sit and wait in two old wooden chairs in front of an old wooden desk. On the desk is a well-used road map of Sri Lanka, spread out and covered with pen marks and circles. There are blank, official Sri Lankan train reservation stubs on the desk, so I think maybe this is legit.

After 5 minutes, I start to get restless and want to leave. The gentleman hovering behind us sees I am losing patience and flips opens an Encyclopedia from the 1960s. He tries to capture my interest by flipping through the pages, pointing to black and white photos, saying, "You look, you look."

Cedric peers over and asks, "Where is that?" The gentleman doesn't answer and continues pushing the book toward me. I won't reach for the book; I don't feel like giving this guy any sort of salesmanship satisfaction.

Finally, the agent arrives and he is all business. He asks us where we want to go. Cedric tells him we want tickets for a later date, starting in the middle of the country. This confuses the agent and he asks, "But how will you travel to this train station?" Cedric explains our well-organised itinerary involving buses and trains. The agent tells us all the trains are booked, there are no tickets left. Helpful.

I make motions to leave. The agent quickly says the train is not the best way to travel because there are so many things to stop and see along the way. He points to the map and says "Here there is a museum, here there is some ruins, here there is a waterfall and the train misses all of these things completely!"

I sit back down. Why would someone selling tickets for the train company try to talk you out of taking the train? He asks us how we are travelling the rest of our trip. Cedric explains the whole itinerary again: the train, the bus, etc. The agent proceeds to tell us the bus is very complicated for tourists, we will have to switch buses many times and that it will be very difficult for us.

We both sit there and look at him, waiting for his sales solution. Nothing. So Cedric asks if there are any tickets available for the last leg of our journey (in January). The guy points over to where we were headed initially, "Oh, you have to check with the reservation office for that." Still not sure what services they offer, we leave the office.

We head to the official reservation area, now only 30 minutes before we have to catch our train. We wait in line and are told that, indeed, train tickets for the most scenic part of our journey are sold out. We snag some 2nd class tickets for our final trip in January and head off to find our train. I ask the man checking tickets where to catch our train. "Fh," he mutters.

I clarify, "Platform four?"

He grumbles, "Fuh!"

I see a faded "4" painted on a small walkway that passes over the train tracks. There is a mass of people waiting on the platform, but some space right at the base of the stairs where we wait. We watch some other trains arrive and there is no clear indication what the wagon classes are. I ask Cedric, "How will we know where the 2nd class seats are?" It's a mad rush whenever a train arrives because the 3rd class seats are first come first serve and everyone else has to stand. I plant the seed of doubt in Cedric's mind and we decide to push through the sea of people and relocate to another part of the platform. Of course, when the train arrives, it is a mad rush and we still have no idea which carriage to enter. I decide to follow a family of white people, assuming they have 1st class seats.

I see a "C" on the side of one carriage and remember seeing that on our ticket somewhere, so I pull Cedric into the C coach. Just like the commuter train station this morning, it is dark. There are absolutely no lights and the aisles are crowded with people. I see a girl with a flashlight, pointing the beam at the wall above the window. She is checking seat numbers. Our seat numbers are much lower than in this cart, so we head to the next. We seem to be going against the flow of traffic. I wait for 6 women to pass me and when no one is courteous enough to let us pass, I rudely shove through the crowd. When in Rome…

Cedric uses the flashlight app on his smartphone and we find our seats. I am happy because the seats have a headrest, a very big window and more legroom than the plane. I look out at the platform still buzzing with people and notice our seats are lined up with the base of the staircase, exactly where we were standing before we moved. Funny how things work out like that.

It takes some time to figure out how to open the large window, but once we start moving, the breeze is very welcome. Passing through the city of Colombo, this time with my eyes open, I see colonial constructions still standing with patches patching patches. There is an interesting mix of new and old.

I soon have to tear my eyes from the hypnotising cityscape because the flashing scenes are making me nauseous. The train bounces in all directions and I realize too late that this mode of transportation may be much, much worse than the bus. I pop a Dramamine and close my eyes, opening them from time to time as we leave the city.

Most of the track north passes through small towns and rice fields. These are not the sprawling fields of North America, flat as far as the eye can see. These emerald patty fields are surrounded by lush, green jungle forests. Occasionally, a lone coconut tree, with its slim trunk gently curving to a staggering height and topped with a round puff of leaves, pops out from this stunning background. I stare at the repeating scene and hope to burn it into my memory forever, but the train sways and I have to close my eyes again. I never really understood what people meant by "cinematic," but this country is exactly that word. I've never experienced anything quite like it.

Every once in a while I open my eyes and see modest mortar houses capped with rippling clay tiles. The dirt roads connecting the homes are a rusty hue. This red beautifully complements the green jungle that is never far. Children run barefoot along these paths and I wonder how they fill their days and what their future holds.

The view is even more stunning with the setting sun, but I dread the approaching night because my eyes haven't had their fill of this movie set come to life. As the sky goes from pink to dusk, the landscape becomes silhouetted and still manages to be beautiful. Looking up, I see enormous bats racing around near the train. They are so fast that you can't focus on them. Right before darkness overtakes, little glowing specs appear—fireflies. Yeah. I'm glad we took the train.

But at four hours travel time (didn't the website say the entire trip was only 4 hours?) I really have to pee. Our smartphone's GPS tells us we are only 2/3 of the way there. We stop often (didn't the website said this was a non-stop express train?) but all the announcements are in Sinhalese, so we don't know what is happening. Later we determine these are snack and bathrooms breaks.

TIP 21 – You can jump off to pee or get something to eat during train/bus canteen breaks. Just hurry up and remember which carriage is yours!

At one of the stops, I see some mosquitoes. I mention that I'm getting bit and Cedric says, "Oh yeah, I think there's malaria here." Say what, now? Paranoid, I swat at my arms and legs for the rest of the ride. Will be looking for some DEET tomorrow.

TIP 22 – The risk for malaria is indeed present in the north of the country, but it is still a very, very small risk, almost nonexistent, probably less than a fraction of a fraction of a percent. Malaria is transmitted by a type of mosquito that bites at night, particularly in deep forested area (i.e. on a train passing through jungles). Antimalarial drugs are usually not recommended as the risk is too low. The general recommendation is to apply DEET to prevent mosquito bites, particularly if you are in a rural area, in the north of the country. This is merely an opinion and not an official recommendation, you should consult a doctor and/or do your own research.

Exiting the train at Anuradhapura station, we accept a ride from a tuk tuk to the guesthouse. I like this young driver and think I should take his phone number to use his services, but I am dopey from my Dramamine and forget to ask him.

TIP 23 – If you come across a tuk tuk driver you like, ask for his number for future use in the city.

The Lievis Tourist Homestay is motel-style, L-shaped and single level. Each room door opens onto a covered area with little tables and chairs. A 30-something white man sits at one of the tables, typing on his laptop. This seating area is brightly lit and crawling with flying insects. The owner and an employee open the motel door behind the laptop guy and explain this is our room. There are hundreds of dead mosquitoes on the floor at the entrance of this room. With the door open, the owner shows us the attached bathroom, explaining the hot water system and yells something to his employee in Sinhalese. The employee comes back with an aerosol can and proceeds to spray down the bathroom and bedroom. Smells like peaches, it must be similar to what they sprayed on the plane. It kills mosquitoes on contact. The employee finally sweeps the dead mosquitoes out of the room and we are alone.

I am overjoyed to have an attached, private bathroom. The shower has hot water and the beds are comfortable. The room is fairly large, with a desk/table and power adapters provided. There is a large drying rack and overhead fan. I love this place.

DAY 3: DECEMBER 20, 2014

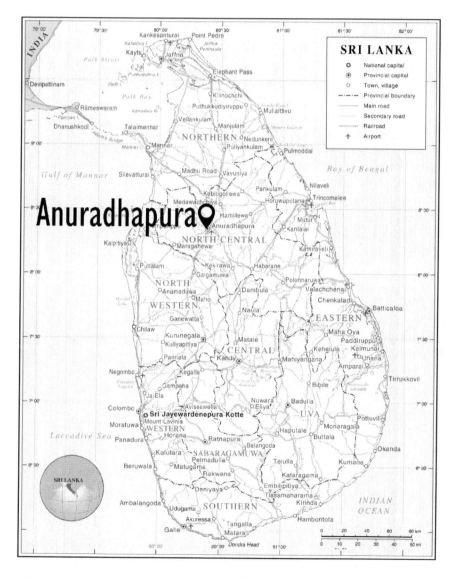

We get up at around 9 am and go to the front desk to ask if they serve breakfast. To my surprise, not only do they serve breakfast, but it's included in the price of the room. I'm really going to have to get used to this. We sit down and they quickly start serving food. They bring omelette, fresh fruit and tea. Very similar to our previous guesthouse actually. Again, delicious.

TIP 24 – If you plan on eating at the hotel, ask what time they serve meals. Some have quite restricted times.

Today we want to go visit the ruins of Anuradhapura. The entrance ticket is 3,250 rupees per person and we require a tuk tuk to drive us around the ruins as they are very spread out. Normally, we could easily rent a bike to do this but guess what? It's raining. The tuk tuk costs us 2,000 rupees, which makes the whole day at Anuradhapura a total of 8,500 rupees (around $85). Extremely expensive; it's about a month's salary in this country.

TIP 25 – The Anuradhapura ruins are very peaceful and pleasant. Rent a bicycle to tour them if it's not raining. Your guesthouse will be able to arrange anything you need, whether you want to rent bicycles or hire a tuk tuk or even a car. They make a commission from the sales of these services, it's a very big business in small towns like Anuradhapura. If you're on a budget, always try to negotiate.

At the ruins, a lot of the roads are flooded and the driver has to turn around, so we don't see many of the sites. We visit a lot of "Stupa" structures and a big Buddha statue.

The day is fun and quite an experience. This "lost city" existed more than 1,000 years ago and was discovered by the British some 60-70 years ago. It was restored and a lot of the monuments are still used today for religious ceremonies.

I make our trip sound bad so far; it's actually quite an experience and I am absolutely happy to be having it. For someone like me, who has never been in a poor country, I must say everything is overwhelming. Before coming to Sri Lanka, I thought Thailand was a relatively poor country. In perspective, Thailand is crazy rich compared to Sri Lanka.

I enjoyed my day at the ruins, but was it worth the close to $100? Absolutely not. We go back to the hotel and have supper there. We order a typical vegetarian Sri Lankan meal. It comes with rice, dal, hot sauce and some other things I don't remember, it was actually pretty good.

TIP 26 – Unless you are in a bigger city, eating at the guesthouse will be your best option. They usually make decent to excellent food

that's also inexpensive.

We go to bed. Did I mention it's raining?

DAY 3: SARAH'S TAKE

People chatted at the tables outside our room until midnight last night. While I was lying in bed trying to sleep, I realized that I was so taken with the scenery that I only took one picture of our train ride.

This morning's omelette was quite salty, but still delicious. The mountain of toast is cold and barely toasted. Cedric jokes that they probably just re-heat leftover toast and that's why they can't brown it too much. Again, I am delighted to be brought a big pot of coffee.

The host asks us our plan for the day. We say we want to visit the ancient city of Anuradhapura. He tells us it is very big and better to rent a bike, but since it is raining we should hire a driver. He offers to get us a tuk tuk for the day, Cedric asks how much and he says 2,000 rupee. We find this expensive, but it's raining so much we can't even walk into town to find a better price. Stranded, we accept the offer. I regret not asking for the phone number of our tuk tuk driver last night.

I ask our host where to buy rain gear. He talks about a clothing store in town and tells us he will tell the tuk tuk driver to take us there before the ruins. I ask about mosquito spray and he explains that they use essential oil lotions to repel bugs, not spray chemicals.

TIP 27 – The essential oil repellents available in Sri Lanka don't work. Bring DEET from home. Many companies make wipes/towelettes if you your flight has a liquid ban.

The tuk tuk driver arrives quickly and our host instructs him to take us to buy umbrellas and bug repellant. The driver is a quiet older man. He drives us to a department store where Cedric and I buy matching striped umbrellas. I tell him I want to get bug repellant next and he tells us the bug repellant is at the grocery store and we can pick it up after we visit the ruins. I always find it annoying when I'm paying for a service, but I don't get to dictate the terms of said service. I wanted the repellant for today because we are outside all day, but there won't be many bugs in the pouring rain, so I don't insist.

Our first stop inside the ancient city is a large, colonial building. We buy our tickets from a grumpy woman and tour inside the building. We see some Buddhist artifacts from the area, dating back over 2000 years, and learn about how the British discovered the ruins and reconstructed some of the structures. Heading back to the tuk tuk, the driver takes us to a reconstructed stupa.

Walking toward the enormous round structure, we soak our shoes by stepping in a huge lake of rainwater. Stupas often house the remains of Buddhist monks and are used as a place of meditation. Cedric tells me we aren't allowed to wear shoes on the site anyway and suggests we just take them off. We roll up our pants and trudge through the puddles. We circle the stupa, there isn't much to see, but I love walking barefoot on these smooth stones. Something about it feel freeing. Back at the tuk tuk, the driver tells us we should remove our shoes and leave them with him. Would have liked him to suggest that before we soaked them, but holding an umbrella and camera, it's nice to not have to carry them.

We drive until a river blocks our path; the road overtaken with flowing water. A police truck pulls in front of us. Some people step out and wade through the current. Once the tuk tuk driver sees how deep the water rises up their legs, he turns around.

He drives down another path until the river overtakes this road too. During our search for a road that doesn't end in a river, I'm surprised to see houses that people are living in. Isn't this an archeological/religious site? Little kids are out playing in the flooded roads. I have to give our driver props; he absolutely tried every road, but they were all flooded. We are restricted to an incredibly small area of the site. The entire ancient city measures 40 km^2, but we see less than a quarter of it and miss lots of stuff included in our ticket price.

Visiting a newly rebuilt stupa, we start to see more locals; dressed in white and making offerings. Cedric is yelled at for wearing a baseball cap in front of the Buddha—oops. Our driver takes us to a huge stupa which is full of barefoot locals. Here we see signs that say, "As a sign of respect, please wear light coloured clothing" and "Please remove your shoes." We are unsure about taking pictures, so we try to be quick and discreet.

TIP 28 – When visiting Buddhist sites, they ask that you don't wear dark clothing (disrespectful), shoes or hats. So bring a bag to carry your hat and shoes if you will be biking. Light shoes (flip flops) are better since they are lighter to carry and easier to slip on and off.

As this is a Buddhist site and there are food and flower offerings, we see monkeys, cats and dogs hanging around. It feels a bit weird to be gawking and taking pictures while people are performing religious ceremonies. We visit a tree planted by Buddha, and sacred stone mountains and caves. While I'm not sure of their exact significance, I enjoy the day outside. When we have visited all there is to see, and our fingers and toes are completely wrinkled, I am very ready to leave in our tuk tuk.

As promised, we stop at the grocery store. Our feet are too wet and muddy to put on our shoes, so we enter barefoot. They have a sign that you have to wear shoes and we get some looks, but no one says anything. The thrill of this little rebellion makes me a little giddy. We buy shampoo, soap, repellant, water, snacks, etc.

TIP 29 – Stock up on water and nuts or dal/mung bean snack at the grocery store because supper at the guesthouse is often served after 8 or 9 pm. Depending on where you are from you may be used to eating at this time (or not).

As we are waiting in line at the cashier, I see our tuk tuk driver walking down the street. I am not surprised to find our tuk tuk empty when we return. I tell Cedric it is a good thing we brought our bag into the store because it contains passports, camera, money, etc. The driver in the neighbouring tuk tuk looks at us incredulously as we hop in the empty tuk tuk.

Our driver returns with a bag from the bakery, explaining he just stepped out to get something to eat. I guess it was quite a long day for him too. Maybe we should have bought him something to eat. We return to the guesthouse and give our driver a 200 rupee tip. He takes the money and plods over to the office…giving the owner his cut, I presume.

We are soaked from visiting the ruins, so I lay everything out on the drying rack and turn the overhead fan to high. I apply some mosquito repellant and we sit at the table outside our room to eat the guesthouse's vegetarian curry.

TIP 30 – Vegetarians/vegans will be able to respect their diet while travelling in Sri Lanka. Vegetable curries, roti, hoppers and dal (lentil) are staple foods. Just advise your host of your restrictions if you will be eating at the guesthouse.

One order is more than enough for two people: fried rice served with bowls of jackfruit curry, fake meat curry, potato curry, vegetable curry, and spicy onion sambal. Very salty, but tasty (except the jackfruit, that stuff's just weird).

Cedric mentions that no one ever checked our $65 tickets and we could have easily toured the park for free. After a hot shower, I notice the insect repellant doesn't wash off very well and stains the towels.

DAY 4: DECEMBER 21, 2014

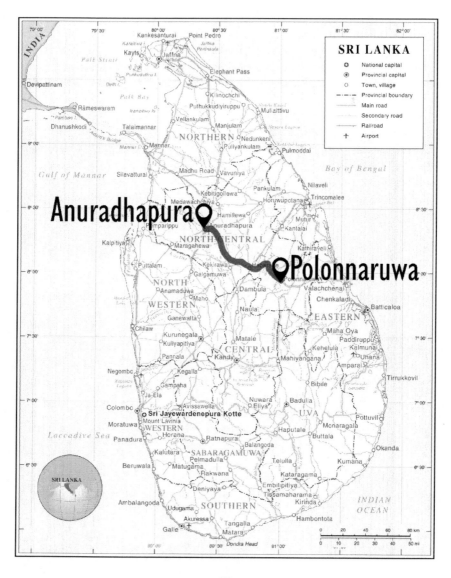

Today we want to go to Polonnaruwa. The owner of the guesthouse is, again, extremely helpful in telling us how to get there, how much it costs, and which bus to take. He calls us a tuk tuk who drives us to the bus station and indicates which bus to take.

We get on the bus and we take a seat. The ride to Polonnaruwa is pretty good. A lot of the roads are flooded and we are lucky the big bus is able to drive through all the water. As we get farther from Anuradhapura the roads are less flooded. I must say the driver drives like a maniac. It is a bit nerve racking at times, but thankfully we get to our destination alive.

Once in Polonnaruwa we take a tuk tuk to Seyara Holiday Resort. The driver managed to fit 4 people on his tuk tuk: 3 in the back, me at the front. Thankfully the hotel is only a 5-minute drive. He points out two monkeys copulating at the side of the road and we share a laugh.

The driver offers to take us around the ruins which are, again, quite spread apart. He quotes us 2,000 rupees. That would make it yet another $85 day. This time I tell him that I can't do it because it's too much. So he replies, "How much can you pay?"

I tell him, "1,000 rupees."

To which he tells me there is no way he can do it for such a low price. He continues and says, "1,800 rupees is my lowest price." I think about it a little bit and I say yes. After all, we didn't come all this way to not see the ruins. And since—guess what?—it's raining, there is no other way to do it than by tuk tuk. So I tell him ok.

TIP 31 – Even in small towns, never feel like there is only one tuk tuk offer on the table. Your best bet is to get a couple of quotes, from different drivers and your guesthouse owner. Sometimes the tuk tuk driver will offer a better price than your guesthouse and vice versa.

Before we go to the ruins, we need to eat. I look on TripAdvisor and find a restaurant that is rated #1 in Polonnaruwa: Priyamali Gedara Farmer Lunch. We ask our tuk tuk driver to take us there, but he doesn't want to. Which I found very strange. He says, "Why don't you eat at your hotel? They have a good restaurant."

Sarah and I look and each other and don't really know what to reply to that. Why does it matter to the taxi driver where we eat? Besides if he needs to take us to another destination, he makes more money. I end up telling him, "Ok, so we call another taxi for going to the restaurant?"

To which he says, "Ok, I will take you." But he was really upset still that we didn't eat at our hotel. He kept asking us again, "Why don't you eat at your hotel? It's good."

Sarah reassures him, "We will eat there tonight and tomorrow. Today we just want something different." He seems to understand this and calm down.

So he takes us to the restaurant and he tells us we can pay him later for this small trip, which is worth 100 rupees. We get to the restaurant and to our surprise it is a buffet. We are in a small hut and there are 10-15 dishes in the middle. Our plates are banana leaves, we get up and the owner shows us what all the options are. I have some dal, rice and some other things, the food is stone cold. It tastes ok, but nothing extraordinary. For desert there are pineapples and small cakes. It's alright, but we don't find it worth a #1 restaurant. It's a nice local food experience nonetheless.

I ask for the bill and they slap us with a 2,000 rupee bill (around $20). I look at Sarah in desolation. 2,000 rupees for a little bit of rice and lentils? This is an incredible amount of money in this country. We just got robbed again. Same thing in Thailand would be around $1.50. The funny thing is before we left for Sri Lanka, we treated ourselves with a 5-star meal in Thailand. It was absolutely amazing and some of the best food I've had in a long time. The price for a 5-star meal for 2 people in Thailand was $20.

TIP 32 – No matter what it is (restaurant, tuk tuk, souvenir) always ask "How much?" beforehand. Every time we forget to do this, the bill is staggering.

We keep paying first world prices in this developing country. I must admit, it is quite surprising. We are on a budget and we picked Sri Lanka as a travel destination because we thought it would be super cheap. For what you get, it is turning out to be one of the most expensive countries in the world. It is either as much or more money than Canada/US. Our days are costing us, including hotel, transportation, food and activities, around $200 per day, which will equal around $4,000 at the end of our 20-day trip. We thought it would cost less than half that, around $2,000 maximum. So right now we are admittedly, quite depressed.

What is the most frustrating in all this is that we pay first world prices, but the state of this country is dismal. The tuk tuks are in disrepair, the trains are the same ones that were built 70 years ago, the mains roads are paved, but as soon as you turn off a main road, they are all dirt roads, very bumpy and full of holes. So it makes you wonder, where is all this tourism money going? The tuk tuk drivers are making an incredible amount of money, yet their vehicles are barely working.

Oops, went out on a rant there. Where were we? We just finished eating at the expensive buffet. We call our taxi driver and tell him we are ready to go visit the ruins. He picks us up very quickly. I tell him we need to stop at an ATM first. He says no problem. He stops at an ATM but the transaction fails. He brings us to another ATM, our card fails again. Brings us to another one, fails again. Our driver introduces us to another tuk tuk, so we go ahead and switch tuk tuk. Our old driver doesn't even ask to be paid for any of it. He drove us around the whole town to all the ATMs; very strange.

We try different debit and credit cards at all the machines, but they all fail. We visited all the ATMs in town. It can't be our bank because we are trying all our cards, even MasterCard fails to work. We are stuck, we don't have enough money to visit the ruins, which amounts to 8,500 rupees ($85) including the tuk tuk.

Our new driver wants to take us to his friend's woodwork shop. He says if we have MasterCard we can buy a 1,000 rupee wood art and the merchant will pass the transaction at 10,000 rupees and give us the change (9,000 rupees). It seems a bit fishy and, at this point, we are just tired of spending a fortune every day. We tell him to just drop us off at our hotel. Disappointed, he says ok.

But 5 minutes later, guess where the tuk tuk stops? At his friend's woodwork shop. Sarah, trying to remain calm, attempts to communicate that we couldn't care less about this shop and just want to go to our hotel. He insists it's like a museum and we should go check it out. We don't bulge and stay in the tuk tuk. After 3-4 minutes of trying to convince us, he obliges and drives us the hotel. What a day! This town was just a very bad experience for us. We go to the hotel and eat there (our tuk tuk driver would be pleased). Again, a typical Sri Lankan meal. It was ok, but not great. I think we're done trying Sri Lankan food at this point, and look forward to leaving tomorrow. Did I mention it's raining?

DAY 4: SARAH'S TAKE

I had a terrible sleep. Chatty guys were outside at the table again last night. When they finally quieted down, I got up for a last bathroom trip. As I fought to escape the mosquito netting and swung my legs down from the bed, my foot grazed *something* on the floor that disappeared under the bed. Creatures in the dark creep me out. I couldn't sleep afterward because I was imagining every possible animal. (But mostly: snake, snake, snake!) After an hour or two, I finally summoned the courage to lower myself to the floor and shine the phone's flashlight under the bed...tiny frog.

I left the fan on high all night, but our things are still damp this morning. I pack them up with hope that they might dry out at the next place.

We eat the same breakfast of omelette, fruit, toast, and a large pot of tea for Cedric and coffee for me. Since he doesn't handle caffeine very well, and I am a caffeine addict, I drink most of Cedric's tea. It is foolish to drink so much liquid before a long bus ride, but I just can't resist the free caffeine.

Cedric takes a sip of the tea and he is impressed. "Oh, that's good," he says. Perhaps it's because I'm no tea expert, but I can't distinguish between this Ceylon tea *de terroir* and the Lipton's 200 pack I get on sale at Costco back in Canada. I'm kind of embarrassed that I don't notice a difference, so I just respond with a noncommittal but agreeable, "Mmm. Right?"

We are eating earlier than yesterday and all the guests are out and the tables are full. We are seated closer to the trees and we see a couple of hummingbirds and squirrels as we enjoy our breakfast. Because of the constant rain and mosquitoes, I never noticed that the yard is very nice and peaceful.

After we eat, the guesthouse owner arranges for a tuk tuk to take us to the bus station. It costs 250 rupee. It is about the same distance as the train station and more than double what our first driver charged us. So I presume our host's cut is about 50%.

We get on the empty bus and have our choice of seats. As a North American, I would approximate this to a school bus. It is nothing like a city bus and not even close to a coach. Bright blue curtains cover the windows from the glaring sun. Colourful Buddhist images and other religious paraphernalia decorate the bus and it has a festive spirit.

TIP 33 – If you want a seat on the bus, you need to embark at the start of the route and get there early.

As more people board the bus, vendors start to appear in the aisles. They are selling fried snacks, and toys that spin and light up. One hands out children's books that he later passes by to collect; whoever wants to keep them, pays him at that time. There is a male singer with a tambourine that slowly walks the aisle serenading us. He isn't bad. People are giving him coins, so Cedric drops a 20 rupee note in his basket when he passes us. A man comes around and asks us where we are going. Cedric tells him Polonnaruwa and he tells us 150 rupees each and hands us our tickets. Pretty good price, 300 rupees for a 100 km journey.

The driver blasts Indian pop music through an amped up sound system, lights up some incense and sets off on the journey. We are seated under a speaker, so with the music, the smell and the heat, I am feeling overstimulated and I need to pop another motion sickness pill. I close my eyes and settle in for a long journey.

It's not long before Cedric elbows me and motions out the window. We have stopped and I see water covering the street. Up ahead is a small bridge that would normally pass over a trickle of a stream. Today there is no ground, only water.

As we leave the city, the devastation is worse. I see a woman standing on the side of the road, staring back at a house in 2 feet of water. I don't know if this area is normally plains or farmland because all we can see is a muddy river. Over the road and as far as I can see, everywhere is rushing water. Not a lake; a moving river with a strong current. We pass more flooded houses. The bus is quite high off the ground and we drive through currents that many vehicles cannot. After kilometers of this heavily flooded area, I start to see the road again and the water in the fields becomes more still. When the road is dry, we see crowds of people, bicycles, motorbikes, tuk tuks, cars, trucks, vans, tractors, police officers, and ambulances waiting at the shore of where the strong current begins. How long will they wait? I am so grateful this bus made it through the water. Grateful to be only a visitor here, that it was not my house submerged.

For the rest of the trip, I occasionally open my eyes and see that many board at the various stops and a lot of people are standing. I'm so glad that we are seated.

TIP 34 – If you visit during a rainy season, consider that these large, high buses are the only vehicle that can drive through deep water. A private car or smaller air conditioned bus aren't high enough off the ground.

From our train ride experience, I know there will be snack/pee breaks. A teenage boy sits down next to Cedric and starts chatting. He's very friendly and probably likes practicing his English. When the bus stops, he tells Cedric, "Canteen."

I ask the young man, "Is there toilet and how long will we stop?" He says there is a toilet, but doesn't understand the rest. Despite my dopiness, I remember to pocket some toilet paper and run off to find the bathroom, not knowing when the bus will be leaving.

TIP 35 – Ladies, always have toilet paper/tissues in your pocket. Handwashing stations are no guarantee either, so bring hand sanitizer. If the plane won't let you travel with liquid, bring sanitizing wipes.

I am quite out of it from my Dramamine and just keep following the crowd down a long, narrow stretch of broken concrete into a jungle. I see a rundown shack and find the women's side. When I enter, there is a woman squatting and she quickly reaches to close the door. Squat toilets are never a picnic. Luckily, my pills have made me relaxed enough that I don't think about it. I enter the stall, try to close the door (no lock), and just hold the door closed with one hand. I am not well-practiced with squat toilets. I imagine there is a technique, like anything else, involving angles and aim. Having once accidentally doused my pant leg with poor aim, I've been quite deliberate since then. Pants are the real pain. I imagine squat toilets are one reason why every woman wears a skirt in this country. Normally, if I have a stall to myself, I will remove my pants entirely. There's no room here, so I tightly bunch my clothes at my knees, hold the stall door closed and balance myself. I successfully pee (none on myself) and feel immense relief. There is an old bucket sitting underneath a crusty tap, so I "flush" my waste down the hole and get the heck out of there, thinking, "Hand sanitizer, hand sanitizer."

Highly impressed with myself and how well I did in the squat toilet, I hold my head high and walk confidently back to where the buses are parked. Loud honking and an announcement in Sinhalese spikes my anxiety and I take off at a run—to the amusement of people at the canteen—like only a foolish white person can, terrified the bus will leave without me. I arrive to the parking lot and see three identical buses. While each bus has its destination written on the front, it is Sinhalese script and I didn't memorize the characters. I eventually find my bus and happily take my seat next to Cedric. Seeing I'm a little out of breath and panicked-looking, he raises an eyebrow, "Everything okay?"

After a 2+ hour journey, the guy who sold us our ticket comes to tells us the next stop is Polonnaruwa. There is no announcement, so I guess most people know where to get off. Of course, we've only paid up to this point and they need the seats, but I am still very happy to have someone advising us. We hop off on a quiet city street with other tourists and immediately surrounded by tuk tuk drivers. From all sides, you hear, "Where you going, sir?" Cedric tells an older man with about three teeth to his name where we are staying and asks if he knows it. He says, "Yes, follow me."

Cedric asks him several times, "How much?"

As we near his tuk tuk, he finally answers, "200." Right next to his tuk tuk, Mr. Three-teeth says, "I just need to drop off these people first. They are on the way."

A young Japanese couple pile into the back of the tuk tuk with their suitcases. I also get in the back with my backpack and don't understand where Cedric will fit. Normally, tuk tuks fit two people in the back with small bags or three people with no bags and there is a single seat in the front for the driver. Mr. Three-teeth seats himself up front. He pats the framework that secures his seat to the tuk tuk and motions for Cedric to sit on it. Cedric balances himself here, holds on tight and chats with the driver.

Upon arrival at the guesthouse, the host welcomes us. He wants us to sit and offers some tea because the room is not ready, but we are rushed to go to the #1 TripAdvisor restaurant and we don't stay.

Our driver brings us to the restaurant at 12:50 and says he'll pick us up at 2:30. I think that's way too long, but two women with umbrellas quickly usher us out of the tuk tuk. They lead us to a mud hut with a woven grass roof. There is no sign or menu or anything. Benches line the walls and long, narrow tables are set up in front of the seats. In the middle of the hut is a table loaded with dishes. I spot a framed TripAdvisor Certificate of Excellence hanging on a beam. There's two other couples and a family of four all eating in this large hut. All the patrons are white.

A girl asks us what we want to drink and I ask her what they have. My stomach is upset from the bus ride, so I take the "ginger beer." She goes to get our drinks and tells us to serve ourselves. As we are at the table, the owner walks over and welcomes us loudly. Then he takes us through each dish: mango curry, jackfruit curry, eggplant, chicken, dal, roti, rice, etc. The food is pretty good. Since it's been sitting out for who knows how long, I don't venture into the meat dishes, sticking to vegetable, lentils and roti. There is fresh fruit, fried banana fritters and buffalo curd for dessert. I have heard about this buffalo curd dessert served in a little clay dish and am intrigued, but I don't want to insult the host if I don't like it, so I don't try any.

Cedric and I are the last to arrive and after we serve ourselves, the food dishes are carried back to a house behind the hut. About 5 minutes later, the dishes are paraded back out to an identical hut next to ours. There's ten new white tourists about to dig into our leftovers. I am delighted by my drink choice. The ginger beer is awesome: not too sweet, fizzy, fresh ginger flavour with a pleasant spicy note.

TIP 36 – Try the Elephant House Ginger Beer (EGB) as early in your trip as possible. Delicious and soothing for the digestive system, they sell it most places.

My happiness over the discovery of this soft drink is dampened when we get the bill and are astounded by the total. The price wasn't posted and we should have asked. Every time we don't ask "How much?" before, the bill is always astronomical. Their receipt boasts the TripAdvisor logo in the top-left corner.

It is 1:20 and we don't want to wait another hour for our tuk tuk, so we ask the owner if he knows our driver's phone number. He does! Owner dials him and passes me the phone, I tell him we are done and ask him if he can pick us up. He says 10 minutes.

I tell Cedric that I don't want to visit anything and that I just want to go back to the hotel. Yesterday's visit in Anuradhapura was very expensive and today's lunch was another surprise cost. Cedric kind of ignores my suggestion and tells the driver we need to visit an ATM before the park. The whole day will cost close to $100 and we don't have much cash left.

The first ATM we visit looks to be about 30 years old. I enter my card and pin, taken to the screen to select my account and amount. At the point in the process where the machine would spit out the money, it beeps and says transaction declined. We tell the driver and he doesn't seem surprised. He takes us to several other ATMs and none of them work with my card. I was trying to take out the maximum withdrawal amount and realized maybe the machines don't allow that much cash to be taken out in this small and dingy town. At the last one, I try lowering the withdrawal amount. Still declined.

From the tuk tuk driver to our restaurant experience to the ATMs, I dislike this town. I just want to sleep the day away and hope for better in the next place. I try again to tell Cedric this town is no good. We should take the dysfunctional ATMs as a sign, call it a day and return to the hotel.

So far we've just tried my bank card at the ATMs because Cedric left his back at the hotel. Since Cedric successfully used his ATM card at the airport, he thinks his card might work. So the driver takes us back to the hotel, Cedric gets his card and we return to the first ATM. I stay in the tuk tuk and take a look around. We are back where the bus dropped us off this morning, the street lined with tuk tuks.

The driver, Mr. Three-teeth, has a real frantic energy about him, like he is always in a hurry to get somewhere. I find this strange because we hired him for the day and, being his only client, our schedule should be his schedule. As soon as Cedric steps into the bank, the driver gets on his phone. Still on his phone, he leaves me and walks across the street where he initially picked us up, toward some other tuk tuks. I stop paying attention to him and focus on trying to change my attitude so that I can enjoy the rest of this day.

I see the driver walking back to me with another Sri Lankan. Will we be splitting the ride again? "Hello, madam," the new stranger greets me with a huge grin. This guy, 20 years younger and in full possession of his teeth, peers into the back of the tuk tuk where I'm seated and our tuk tuk driver sits down in his seat.

He turns toward me and puts on his matter-of-fact voice, "Now, madam."

I think, "Oh no, here we go." I listen intently because I am on high b.s. alert.

Three-teeth pulls out an old-school cell phone from his shirt pocket. "Now, madam," he starts again, opening his calendar application. He swears and fiddles some more until he opens the calculator function. "Now, madam," he says for a third time. "You are going to spend 6,500 rupees for the tickets." He punches this information into the calculator. "Then it will cost you another 1,800—" he stops himself. "It should have been 2,000 rupees, but you negotiated a lower price and I can see you are good people, so I accept at 1,800 rupees." Since I am fully aware of this negotiation, I can only assume this summary is for his friend. "Then for all the driving around I did, to the lunch and ATMs, another 500 rupees. This brings your total to 8,800 rupees." He shows me his cell screen with the calculator screen showing 8800. I don't say anything. "Now, madam, if you go with my friend here, he will include the cost of the ticket and all the tuk tuk rides for 7,000 rupees."

This doesn't make any financial sense, so I know there is a catch. Still working out his puzzle, I stall, "First, we need to get money. Then we can think about this offer. Right now, we do not have 7,000 rupees."

He says, "Of course, madam. Of course."

Cedric returns and says ATM didn't work for him either. Three-tooth informs Cedric we will go with this new driver now. Three-tooth is so eager to be rid of us, he doesn't even explain his calculations to Cedric.

Cedric tells me he tried all his cards, including his credit cards, and none of them worked. In French, I tell Cedric that our drivers are offering to "include the cost of the ticket." But similar to what we realized in Anuradhapura, no one checks the tickets, so they will not buy any tickets, hope no one stops us and keep all of the money for themselves. Instead of making 1,800 rupees to drive us around, they make 7,000.

I actually don't mind this arrangement. Obviously, I would only pay at the end. If we get caught without a ticket, we just go buy it at 6,500 rupees and the driver makes only 500. If we don't get caught, I'll probably argue that he didn't buy any tickets and only pay him the 500. Of course, I would finally settle at the initial 1,800—man's got to make a living and I respect that—but it's always better to mitigate disappointment. Either way, it's cheaper than expected, and this lightens my mood.

Before anything, we need to get money out of an ATM. This isn't a credit card nation and we need cash to live out our next three weeks here. I keep telling Cedric that it's just this terrible town and we'll probably get a working ATM in the next city.

While Cedric is visiting yet another ATM, the driver asks me if we have a credit card. I am hesitant to answer this. I avoid his question and say we've tried all the cards and ask him if all tourists have this problem. He answers yes in a way that makes me think he doesn't know what I asked. He keeps asking about the credit card. I don't see the harm and am curious to know what he's thinking, so I tell him that we do, but that it doesn't work here (thinking back to TGI Friday's in Colombo). He gets excited and tells me he knows how we can get money.

He explains how we can go visit his friend's wood factory, buy a little something, pass the card for more and get the rest in cash. I slowly and deliberately say no. I explain that our credit card doesn't work and that if this last ATM doesn't work, we will go back to the hotel. I tell him that we traveled all day, are tired and just want to go to the hotel. I repeat that if this ATM doesn't work, we will go back to the hotel and try again tomorrow.

Cedric returns and says none of the cards work. I tell the driver to take us back to the hotel. He is resistant, but I push and he says OK. On the way back, I explain to Cedric in French the nonsense about the wood factory. It seems like the driver is taking us in wrong direction, but I arrived only 4 short hours ago, so what do I know?

The driver stops at the side of the road and kills the engine. He hops out of the tuk tuk and says, "This is wood shop, you can take out money here."

Annoyed to go through this again, I tell him, "No. We don't want to. Just take us to the hotel."

His friend comes out of the shop with an umbrella and walks toward the tuk tuk. Smiling he greets us warmly, "Hello! Come inside."

Cedric can tell how annoyed I am and tries to take over before I snap. He waves his hand and tells them, "No, no, we don't want to." We don't get out of the tuk tuk. "No, we don't want to," Cedric repeats.

They don't budge either and the shop owner says, "Come, come inside. We have very nice wooden animals, elephants."

I tell him, "No, thank you. We are going to our hotel."

They both peer into the backseat at us, the open door flap comically framing their persistent faces. The driver smiles at me and says, "It is like a museum, madam. Come inside."

I say, "No. Take us to the hotel."

He stays planted outside the tuk tuk, still trying to convince us. How long will this standoff go on? We are on some deserted road, who knows where, and I am feeling powerless, which makes me angry. I hate this shabby town, with no working ATMs and scammers everywhere you look. First, Mr. Three-teeth, then Mr. Pricey-buffet, now these two grinning sharks. I want to explode at them, but I don't know if that could put us in danger. Would they be violent toward us? Would they try to nick our passport? So I try a different tact.

I relax and smile at the driver, "Do you know the name of our hotel?"

Proud men like to show off. He happily affirms, "Yes."

I ask, "What is it?"

He sits down in his driver seat, thinking and says, "Seyara."

I happily exclaim, "Yes, that's it!" I pause, tap his shoulder twice and firmly say, "I want you to take us there. Now."

To my great surprise, he starts the engine. He turns the tuk tuk around and drives slowly by the shop. Pointing to a wooden statue outside the shop, he says, "This is the largest elephant statue in Sri Lanka."

Another bald-faced lie. I bite my tongue and muster, "Mm-hmm," but can't bring myself to look at it.

We get back to the hotel and I feel bad for the driver. He didn't try to mug us or physically harm us. He is essentially a good person and, like everyone else, just trying to survive in his world. So I say, "Tomorrow we will visit the sites and you can drive us. Does the owner have your number?" I know we will leave for our next destination first thing in the morning, but I want to leave him with some hope.

He says, "No, I don't work with this owner." Interesting. I will pay more attention to the guesthouse-tuk tuk partnerships.

At the hotel, we relax and work until dinner. It is another beautiful yard with mango trees and seats in the garden that would be lovely on a sunny day. A family of British guests get excited about some hummingbirds in the garden. They get their binoculars and start pointing out other birds. I am curious to know what is so interesting about these birds and start to wonder about the animals in Sri Lanka. I've only seen a short documentary about Sri Lankan worker elephants that help move large objects with their trunk and how it is a decreasingly popular trade.

Cedric is researching online and finds another Sri Lankan train company, a private one called Rajadhani Express. They have very luxurious-looking 1st class seats still available to our later destination. He buys train tickets between Nuwara Eliya and Ella. We feel hopeful that we will have a nice, scenic train ride through tea country as this is the quintessential tourist experience in Sri Lanka.

We eat an overly salted meal of chicken curry and rice at the guesthouse. We are offered free coconut cake, which is the most delicious thing we've eaten since arriving in Sri Lanka. The beds are quite short, but at least they have hot water in the shower.

TIP 37 – Unravel and set up the mosquito net over the bed when you arrive at the hotel. Not only does this air them out (often quite musty), but if you wait until night when the mosquitoes are out, you may trap some inside with you.

DAY 5: DECEMBER 22, 2014

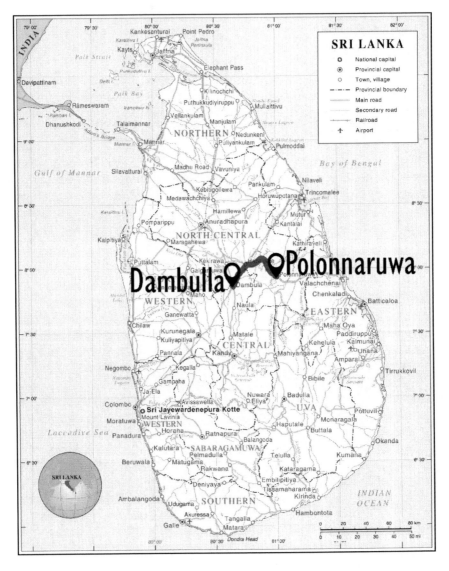

It's a new day. It's time to forget about yesterday and start fresh. Today we want to take the bus to Dambulla. We get up and go sit at the restaurant to eat the breakfast that's included in our room rate. We sit and very quickly, a plate with a fried egg is served for each of us. I don't like fried egg very much, but if it's my only protein source this morning, I have to eat it. I start cutting into it, seems like an odd texture, I touch it. It is stone cold, fresh out of the fridge. I have never seen that in my life, getting served a stone-cold fried egg for breakfast in a restaurant. I can't eat it. I dig into the pile of toast and smother them with strawberry jam and that's it. I'll eat later, I guess.

By the way, every morning so far, we were served 6 toasts for 2 people, along with the egg or omelette. The toasts always have an odd texture and they are not very hot, not very toasted at all, just barely heated up. In every hotel so far, I am pretty sure they reuse the uneaten toasts from the day before. It makes sense, these people are very poor, it would be crazy for them to throw away perfectly good food, so they just put it back in the fridge and serve it again the next day. I'm just glad it hasn't made me sick yet!

We hear a lot of French from the other guests and I realize there are a lot of French tourists here. They are everywhere we go: hotels, restaurants, attractions. It's almost impossible to go somewhere and not hear French.

After breakfast we check out and the owner offers to take us to the main road and help us hail a bus. It's very nice of him to help us, the buses here stop only for a few seconds and you have to hurry up to get on the bus or it might leave without you. So he drives us to the main street. It's only a 2-minute drive, but of course it's raining, so it's nice not to have to walk in the mud. We get out of the car and wait with the guesthouse owner for the bus to come. We wait a good 10-12 minutes until finally a bus comes. The bus is jammed packed. We get on, but there is barely any room to even stand. Sarah finds a spot behind the driver and I have to stand in the door.

Thankfully, the travel time to our destination is not too long, only 1 hour and 20 minutes. (It's only that fast because the driver drives like a maniac.) I've done plenty of 50-minute standing bus commutes in Canada, so I know I can do it.

Being close to the driver is enormously entertaining and the ride passes by in a snap. It is quite something to watch the driver. He basically drives with one hand on the wheel and one hand on the horn. He honks every time we near or pass someone. This is how they drive here, you honk to announce your presence and your intent. I must say I am not a fan of this driving method, I find the horn obnoxious, but in the moment it makes me laugh. Every once in a while the driver prays, joining his hands together. (Thanking god that he is still alive?) If he would just drive a bit slower, this might be a more effective method of staying alive but—who knows?—

maybe his god is very powerful and actually protecting him. I wish it, for everybody's life aboard the bus.

After an hour and twenty minutes, we've finally arrived in Dambulla, alive and well. First thing we want is an ATM. Sarah tries her debit card again and it actually works. Great! Now we have money, we can go to Sigiriya and visit the ruins, but first we want to go check-in at our hotel to drop off our bags.

We grab a tuk tuk and it costs 150 rupees, pretty reasonable, but it's not very far, only 2-3 minutes. We get to the guesthouse and to our surprise, none of the staff speaks English. So the tuk tuk driver stays to assist with translation.

Contrary to all of the other guesthouses we stayed at, where the owner was expecting us, this time the staff has no knowledge of our reservation. They don't speak a word of English, so we try to explain, via the tuk tuk driver's translation, that we have a reservation and that we've already paid. After 10 minutes of discussion, they finally show us a room. About 15 minutes later, someone knocks at the door. It's the owner of the guesthouse and he's asking how we're going to pay for this room. Again, I explain to him that we've already paid through Agoda and I show him my mobile voucher. Having seen a visual proof seems to calm him down a lot. He says he will check with his son to confirm, but he seems to believe us as he is now offering us a cup of tea, which we gladly accept.

TIP 38 – Consider bringing a paper copy of your reservations. While Agoda and other online booking sites claim that you can present an electronic copy of your booking confirmation, we found this doesn't work out at some guesthouses.

After our tea we go to Dambulla Rock Temple. The entrance for this attraction is quite a bit lower than most of the other attractions at only 1,000 rupees. To see the caves you have to climb stairs (maybe 10-20 minutes of climbing depending on your pace), then you are rewarded with a stunning view of mountainous jungle, when it's not raining. Despite today's rain, the view is nice.

At the top there are lots of monkeys and they seem to be the # 1 attraction. Everybody is filming them or taking pictures. I break down and start taking some pictures of them too. The caves themselves are very nice. They display a lot of Buddha statues and paintings on all of the walls. Apparently these paintings are hundreds of years old, I find it quite impressive that this paint is still standing after centuries. Most homes have to redo their paint after at least 20 years. Either the paint was recently retouched or we should analyse what makes this paint so great and become a millionaire selling the best paint in the world.

After a satisfactory 2-hour long visit of the caves, we decide to go eat. TripAdvisor helps us decide on a restaurant called Man J. It's right in the middle of town. By the way, this is a very small town and entirely walkable (if it's not raining), but since it's raining, we decide to take a tuk tuk.

Man J. wasn't great. In fact, it wasn't good at all and we wish we hadn't gone. Sarah noticed a waiter cleaning the table beside us, taking some leftovers from the table and 30 seconds later offering the dish to us for "free." You never really want to be facing the kitchen in a restaurant, do you? She also noticed the waiter cleaning a second table, and this time she witnessed the waiter placing the bottle cap back on an unfinished bottle of beer. These guys really don't waste anything and it puts us off our meal. What else do they not waste that's potentially in our plates? The food is very ordinary, but at least it's our cheapest meal yet, 260 rupees per plate. But the food is not good, so what's the point?

TIP 39 – There are a lot of fake TripAdvisor reviews in Sri Lanka, so take the rave reviews with a grain of salt. A couple places we visited openly offered you discounted or free things to give them a review on the website.

What I have realized is that this country is not a restaurant culture. The population doesn't really eat out at restaurants; the woman stays at home and cooks. So apart from the big cities, Colombo and Kandy, all of the restaurants cater to foreigners, which means all are expensive. There's no "street food" or inexpensive restaurant options in all of the cities we visited so far. By inexpensive, I mean in correlation to the cost of living in this country.

For example, when we visited Bali, we easily found dozens of inexpensive restaurants everywhere we went, offering a meal for $1 to $4. In Thailand, there are literally thousands of street food vendors everywhere you go. You can find delicious food everywhere for under $2. But in most of Sri Lanka, there are no street food vendors, only bad restaurants serving subpar food for 10 times the price it should be. It's basically a scam. Almost every restaurant we go to is around $5 to $10 for a plate. It's an absolute rip-off.

After eating, we walk back to the hotel. Spending 8,000 rupees to visit Anuradhapura, only to see...nothing much, I decide to further research Sigiriya and see if it is really worth the 3,900 rupees per person entrance fee. Well, guess what? An afternoon of research and plenty of pictures, tells me it's not. Sigiriya is basically a big mountain where some king, 1,000 years ago, built his kingdom, protected from attacks on top of the mountain. Today there is almost nothing left to see. Much like Anuradhapura, the ruins are nothing more than a 50 cm-high remnants of walls that were once buildings in this great city. Basically an archaeological site, the entrance fee for this "attraction" is outrageous. They are charging you $40 to climb a mountain. After reading about it all afternoon, we decide to save $100 and not go. We stay in our pitiful hotel room, write and laugh at showering over the toilet.

TIP 40 – Bathroom talk: At the hotels, you generally aren't given toilet paper or a garbage bag in the bathroom. Since you usually don't flush paper, we always keep our plastic grocery bags to use in the bathroom.

DAY 5: SARAH'S TAKE

Tired this morning. Didn't sleep well because I was too cold. Normally this time of year, it would be around 27°C and the thin bedding would be fine, but because of all the rain, it's much cooler. The sheets weren't long enough to cover me, so I wore my warm clothes to bed and tried to huddle, but I was still too cold to sleep well.

Breakfast is another mountain of toasts. I am excited because they are warmer than usual. We are served a tall glass of fresh mango and mixed fruit juices. I think maybe we'll have a nice breakfast! When we are brought the egg, I am a bit disappointed because it is sunny side up and ice-cold with some still transparent egg white. I scrape this raw egg off to the side and eat the rest. Need to have some protein because you never know if the next place will have worse food. Cedric won't touch his. These hosts are kind and I feel it might be rude to leave it untouched (and I also don't want them to serve it to someone else), so I eat a bite of his egg as well. The jam jars have been refilled with unusual jellies and full of crumb and butter remnants.

Yesterday I had laid out our damp clothes to dry, but it doesn't seem to have made a difference. They are starting to take on quite the smell.

It is pouring rain, so the guesthouse owner brings us to the bus stop in his car. He waits with us until the right bus comes. He doesn't talk much to us, but it's incredibly generous of him to wait there with us. When the correct bus comes along, he asks, "Is it OK to stand?" as we are hurried onto the bus by the bus attendants.

It's packed, but I push my way to a spot at the front, right behind the driver. We have to leave our bags next to the driver because we don't have a seat. There is lots of pushing and people trying to overtake your space, so I plant myself firm, hold onto the rail and try not to budge with the pushing. Cedric doesn't take the pushy approach and is stuck on the steps. They always leave the doors open on these buses, so he is barely in the bus at all. He is holding onto the rail, but I am nervous for him. The driver manoeuvres these roads like a maniac: speeding, swerving and braking suddenly. I don't know whether it's the egg or this ride, but I start feeling unwell almost immediately and have to shut my eyes. I open them every time we stop to make sure Cedric and our bags are still there. As soon as there is an open space, I gesture for Cedric to join me in a safer area.

Since we are next to the driver, I can observe his methods. He is constantly honking his horn and talking on his cell phone the whole time. It seems like when we stop, he runs his hands around the wheel and brings them up to his forehead in a kind of spiritual ritual. It's a crazy ride and it passes in a flash.

We get off in Dambulla on the main road. Like Anuradhapura and Polonnaruwa, it's another small city but seems busier. This could be an illusion though, because it only has one main road, so everything is concentrated around it. We spot a bank just across a large-ish traffic circle. Perfect! We don't have to ask for directions.

After I successfully withdraw money from the ATM, we ask a tuk tuk right outside the bank if he can take us to the hotel. He gestures to the tuk tuk next to him and says, "Go him."

So we ask this next driver and he takes us to the Takeshi Inn. It's a short trip down the main road. We arrive and after a confusing exchange with the staff that needs to be translated through our tuk tuk driver, we are shown a room with an attached bathroom.

I am quite down at this point. It's only the beginning of our journey and I want it to be over. I don't want to do anything because everything is so expensive. Cedric convinces me to do the Dambulla Rock Temple because it's pretty cheap and in town. The owner of this hotel is a tuk tuk driver himself and offers to drive us to the temple for 200 rupees. We arrive and I perk up immediately: well-maintained, visually interesting, monkeys, fair price.

At the base of the mountain, there's a huge golden Buddha atop a museum. On the rocks to the side of this museum, there are Buddhist monks statues lined up with offerings. There are lots of monkeys hanging around these orange garbed statues, attracting people and cameras. This museum is not included in the price of the ticket, so we don't enter, but we take pictures like everyone else.

Right where the stairs begin to climb the mountain, we see tons of shoes. We know many Buddhist sites require you to remove your shoes, so I start to unlace my Nikes. A man passing by tells us to keep our shoes and remove them at the top. Glad he told us because it was a good hike to the top of the mountain and it would have been difficult and painful with bare feet. On our climb, there are many vendors stationed on the stairs selling guided tours and all sorts of knickknacks. At the top, there is a little kiosk to check your shoes before entering the caves. It's very inexpensive, like 50 rupees per pair and, like most services in this country, you pay at the end, when you pick up your shoes.

TIP 41 – At the Dambulla Rock Temple, don't take off your shoes at the base of the mountain. Wear them for the climb, your feet will thank you. The sacred space is only a very small fenced area at the top of the mountain.

This rock temple is actually a wonderful experience. They've built a temple exterior in front of the cave entrances.

Sculptures decorate doorways that open to large carved-out rooms in the mountain. It is surprisingly warm and dry in these caves. A welcome feeling after the cool, pervading dampness of the past few days. There are small rooms with large Buddha statues. Large rooms with small Buddha statues. Everywhere, the ceilings and walls are beautifully painted.

The view at the top is outstanding and had it been a clear day, we would have seen the mountain kingdom of Sigiriya.

I really liked this activity. It was not too expensive, close to our hotel and self-paced. We were offered the services of a guide several times, but we refused and could simply tour the site on our own. Most of our other activities were reliant on a driver which always feels like we need to adjust ourselves to their schedule.

Atop the mountain, Cedric finds us a well-rated restaurant on TripAdvisor and after we climb down, we hire a tuk tuk from the temple to take us there. The driver says 400, but I tell him I can call my driver and get it at 200. He accepts 200. It's much easier to negotiate when you know a realistic price. The driver claims to know the restaurant, but we drive all around town. It surprises me that he struggles to find it because the town only has one main street and not that many restaurants. After asking several passersby, we find it and get settled.

It seems OK. I see three tables occupied with Sri Lankans. The fact that it has some local patrons encourages me. We order beer, my favourite EGB ginger beer and two dishes. The table behind Cedric clears out and when they leave, I see our server pick up a small bowl from their table. He walks back to a piles of clean dishes, wipes out a clean bowl with the filthy dishtowel he has tucked into his apron, and transfers the contents. I say to myself, "No, no, no. Please don't let that be for us."

He approaches our table and presents the bowl, "Here is a little snack. Free." It's a bowl of spiced chickpeas with sliced onions and I must admit that it looks really delicious. Exactly our kind of food. Cedric is delighted...until I tell him what happened.

Our plates arrive and it's way too much food; we should have just ordered one dish. It's looks nice though, so I dig in. The chicken is...odd. I've never had chicken like this before. There is barely any meat on these teeny tiny little bones. The sauce is spicy enough that it masks the odd flavour and texture. I think of all the pigeons I've seen flying around and wonder. Cedric can't bring himself to eat the "chicken" and just eats rice.

TIP 42 – Depending on your appetite, start with one dish and split it (at both restaurants and guesthouses). We found it was always very large portions.

Since this was one of the better TripAdvisor restaurants in the city, we walk to Cargills grocery store for tomorrow's provisions. There isn't any ready-to-eat food, so we just buy some nuts and water. We walk back to the hotel and I spot a nice-looking café on the way back, which could be good for breakfast. (My main criteria always being coffee.) We see cow and calves freely grazing at the side of this main roadway.

TIP 43 – Bathroom talk: Ladies, most of the online advice about

using a "bum gun" is for men. Usually, the bidet sprayer has the best angle between the legs, from the front.

We relax at the hotel. When night falls, there's a lot of mosquitoes in the room, so we stay under the mosquito net on the bed. The net is a bit smelly and has been patched with tape.

DAY 6: DECEMBER 23, 2014

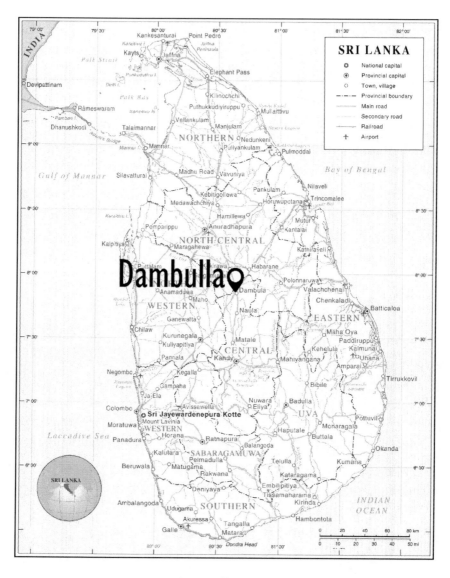

We are very hungry, but have yet to find a restaurant that's worth eating at in this city. I go on TripAdvisor and re-research which restaurant I am going to trust with my health this morning. I find a restaurant that has mixed reviews, but it's the best I can find and only a 7-minute walk from our hotel.

After some morning shopping, we sit at the restaurant and right away the server offers us the buffet for 1,100 rupees per person. I've learnt to stay away from buffets in this country; they are outrageously expensive, usually not very good, have a 50% chance of getting you sick, usually cold, and Sarah and I don't have big appetites enough for it to be worth it.

TIP 44 – Golden rule: stay away from the buffet. Outrageously expensive, usually not very good, and cold. Depending on your appetite, you will rarely eat enough to make it worth your while.

But thankfully, they have an à la carte menu, so we go ahead and order an omelette to share. So far eggs haven't been making us sick in this country, and really, how can you ruin an omelette? So we opt for the safest option, the one that has the best chance of being made fresh. The omelette is actually delicious. We devour it and decide that this restaurant might be worth giving another try for supper. After eating, we have nothing planned. Having done all the research that Sigiriya is really not worth the $100, we decide to not go and actually don't have much to do today. We mostly stay in our room and write.

For supper, we head to the same restaurant. I decide to go with the very expensive 1,100 rupees roasted chicken breast with fries. Having confirmed that their omelettes are actually good, Sarah chooses the cheese omelette. At least if the chicken is inedible, we'll be able to share the omelet. Both of our plates turn out to be delicious and we are very content.

Even though we spent quite a bit for this meal, eating good food is very morally rewarding. Especially now that we are staying in our worst hotel yet. We go back to our hotel and have a relatively good night sleep. Did I mention it's raining?

DAY 6: SARAH'S TAKE

We walk into town and visit the big Benthota bakery for breakfast. It is always really busy whenever we pass by and it's well-rated on TripAdvisor. This tall storefront looks freshly painted black and rusty orange. The bakery is at the front. From what I understand on TripAdvisor, if you walk into the building past the bakery, there is a cheap cafeteria and on the second floor, a more expensive restaurant.

We enter from the street and the bakery is bustling with activity. It's hard to tell if there is a line. There are many people in front of us, so we just stand behind them. I'm trying to see what they have, but the people in front are blocking the view of the glass showcases. We keep waiting, which is fine because we have no idea what to order. As people behind us get served and we are ignored, I think they would let us wait all day. I make eye contact with someone behind the glass, point to a croissant and say, "How much?" He passes us off to a woman who speaks English. I want to ask for a recommendation, but I'm not caffeinated and grouchy. I point to the croissant and a raisin pastry. It's cheap and good.

Next we head to RMS Fashions. I spotted this clothing store when we arrived. It's down an alley off the main road. I had imagined being able to clean my socks and underwear at some point on this trip. Therefore, only brought 7 days' worth of these items. So far, the washing is no problem. But the drying? Not so much. Even if I pay for laundry services, they air dry everything too.

RMS is a really nice-looking store, three floors with big windows. I show the staff my ankle socks and they lead us to the top floor where it is quite dark. Two employees are unpacking boxes with only sunlight to see. Turns out they only have men's socks like these and they cost about $3.50 for 1 pair. I'm not going to buy 13 pair at that price to last me the rest of the trip. Cedric reminds me that we are headed to Kandy next, the second largest city in Sri Lanka. I am hopeful that I will find cheaper things there, so I just buy one pair.

Needing caffeine, we walk to the café I spotted yesterday, closer to our hotel. They have chicken roasting outside on a spit and their menu looks good. I order one coffee. It comes out of a Lipton instant coffee machine pre-sweetened with milk. It's piping hot and does the trick. We sit out on the patio and watch the street life. It's a small town and not much going on.

Today we would have gone to Sigiriya. We visited the temple yesterday, so there isn't much else to do in this town. We are just waiting out the clock until our next destination. It's nice to have time to sit somewhere that isn't the hotel room and I enjoy another mini coffee. A teenager walks by with a baby in her arms. She stops and approaches us with her hand out. I used my last bit of change to buy the second coffee, so I shake my head and tell her, "Sorry." Persistent, she stands there quite a while with her hand out, imploring me with silent eyes. I do feel bad for her. So far, I haven't seen many genuinely happy people in this country.

The café is attached to the Gimanhala Transit Hotel, which has a restaurant that has passed Cedric's TripAdvisor test. It's a lovely restaurant, with nice wooden tables and chairs. It's covered, but open on the sides with a view of the hotel pool and treed yard.

I'm sure there's a view of the mountains too, but it's misty and I can't see them. Although the restaurant itself looks lovely, we are the only customers and I'm highly suspicious. So, I order a pot of tea and Cedric orders the omelette. The eggs are served fresh and hot with some fries and a bit of salad to fill up the plate. Overjoyed that we won't have to eat just peanuts tonight.

We walk back to the inn and relax, writing about our days in Sri Lanka. When it's dinner time, we walk back to the restaurant in the pouring rain. We are rewarded with a good meal and walk back to the hotel feeling better, happy that tomorrow we will be leaving this place.

DAY 7: DECEMBER 24, 2014

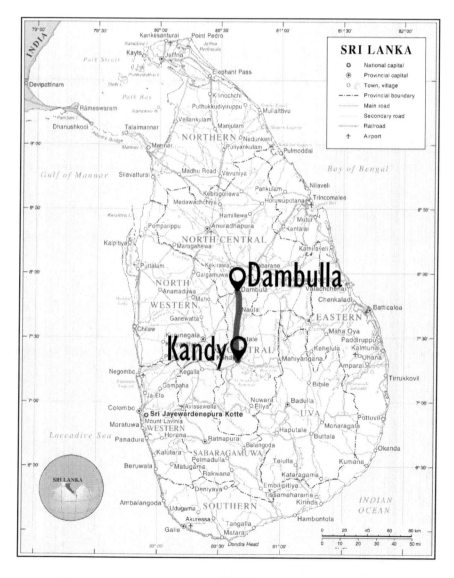

Today is Christmas Eve, but it doesn't feel like it at all right now. Wishing the next hotel will be better than this Takeshi Inn. We are heading to Kandy, the second biggest city in the country. We have hope that returning to civilization will boost our morale. We get up early and aren't that hungry, so we skip breakfast and walk 10 minutes to the town's main bus stop. The ride to Kandy is 2 hours, so we'll just eat when we get there. Technically we could catch the bus by just hailing one just outside our hotel, but hailing a bus is a skill that we don't yet possess. When you hail a bus, you have to be sure it's the right destination. The bus barely slows down, so you have to hop on while it's still moving, which is even harder to do with our heavy backpacks. Furthermore, people usually pile out at the main stop, so that could give us a chance to get a seat.

At the bus stop, it doesn't take long before many buses marked "Kandy" stop. But they are all super full and there is no great flood of people getting off. We wait and hope for an emptier one. After 25 minutes of waiting and seeing dozens of buses pass by, all full, we decide that we'll just catch the next one, even if it's full. Kandy is only 2 hours away, so it doesn't make sense to stand on the street for too long. Might as well stand on the bus and at least we'll be moving.

The next bus arrives and it is a miracle: it's not full. It looks like there might be seats. We hurry up and plunge in the crowd that's trying to get on it. Everybody is pushing to get on the bus first and get a seat. Thankfully, both Sarah and I are able to get a seat, but not together, which is fine. All that matters is sitting. Just getting a seat is a blessing.

While on the bus, I research about Kandy. I find out that Kandy is home to the most modern mall in the country, surprisingly, built by a Thai company, and helped by Malaysian and Singapore engineers. This lifts my spirits. I read that the mall is equipped with a "state of the art food court." Excellent! We'll surely find something edible at this food court.

The bus ride to Kandy is very long and painful. Even sitting ends up being painful after a couple of hours. I later realise that my seat is right above the back wheel of the bus and so it doesn't have any leg room. I have to sit at an angle to put my legs in the aisle, but as the bus fills up, there is barely any room even in the aisle anymore. I am squished and cannot move, it's painful.

Kandy is a city in the mountains. It is highly elevated, around 1 km above sea level, so it's much cooler. As we approach the city, the road curves around the mountains and we go slower and slower. Once in the city, there is a tremendous amount of traffic. It takes an hour to get to the bus station from within the city, almost as long as the trip from Dambulla. It is now noon and we are extremely hungry. So I try to look on my phone's GPS to figure out where we are, to get off the bus close to the mall so we can go eat right away. It's kind of hard to know where we are as the GPS is not very precise at all. But I can see the bus station is a 15-minute walk away from the mall so I resign and just wait for the bus to reach the bus station.

We are in a monstrous traffic jam and have barely moved for the past 20 minutes. As we get closer and closer to the bus station, people just start getting off the bus, we do the same. I recognize where we are and we start heading for the mall. We walk for a while and stop to look at the GPS. But in this country, you cannot stop for even 5 seconds without someone coming to see you to sell you something, most of the time a tuk tuk driver. The problem with tuk tuk drivers is that they want to sell you a tuk tuk ride, so they never tell you 100% accurate information. They always bend the truth (to say the least) so that you will use their service. Anyways, this guy approaches us and asks us where we're going, we try to ignore him but he persists (as they all do), so I tell him we're going to city center mall. He tells me he can bring us there. We tell him we'll walk there so he tells us it's in this general direction. We start heading that way and keep our eyes out for this allegedly "modern mall."

The mall does look relatively modern, it is also relatively small. It has 4 floors but a small area. We quickly walk around the first and second floor but don't see a food court. Sarah thinks it's on the top floor, so up we go. By the way, we cannot find a single directory in the mall.

We arrive on the 4th floor and see a Burger King, that's a very good sign. We walk around the 4th floor in the hope to find the food court. We do indeed find the food court, but it's nothing like we were expecting. Although it's fully built, it's not open. We can see the "state of the art food court" through the glass windows. There are 4 or 5 stainless steel counters and walls with nothing else, no signs, nobody, a big empty area where the chairs and tables are supposed to be. I read that the mall was finished building in 2009...I guess there was not enough business for restaurants to open in the food court? Very strange as the Burger King looks busy as hell. Very hungry now, we resign to eating at Burger King. We order a veggie burger and a chicken burger. It tastes delicious, but as with all fast food chains, it makes our stomach hurt. We grab a few pieces of our candied ginger and instantly feel better.

We get out of the mall and grab a tuk tuk to get to our hotel. Much to our surprise, the hotel is 6 km away, in the mountains surrounding Kandy. But 6 km on these tiny mountain roads is actually quite far. Roads are winding, so it takes a good 15-20 minutes to get there. The driver isn't sure where it is, so we give him the hotel phone number so he can call them.

Side note: it appears like most Sri Lankans are not map friendly. Every time we hire a tuk tuk, I tell him the name of the hotel. Most of the time in small towns the driver knows exactly where it is. But when he doesn't, I show him the map on my smartphone. I have the Agoda app, so it shows on Google map exactly where the hotel is. I show that to the driver but they never, never, never understand it. It's like showing them Chinese. From now on, I simply tell them the name of the hotel and if they don't know it, I give them the hotel phone number.

At the guesthouse we are warmly received with a cup of tea. The owners are very nice and the house is absolutely beautiful. It is a modern looking house, and the cleanest, by far, that we ever stayed in. Our morale just completely turned around (to the positive side). After our cup of tea we are shown to our room. The house is huge. We are going through a maze to get to our room. It's actually very nice, very clean. The bathroom is just outside our room, passed a little living room area. The bathroom actually has a real shower, with a sliding glass door. Simply amazing. Did I mention it's clean?

In the afternoon we just hang out in the living room. There is Wi-Fi and it actually works, and it's fast too.

Around 6 pm the owner comes and asks me if I want dinner. I wasn't sure if they served dinner and I am hungry so I am glad he asked. I gladly say yes, but Sarah says she is not hungry. I think she is lying because we only ate 2 half-burgers for lunch.

It's 8 pm and dinner is served. I am so hungry I could eat an elephant. I go upstairs and sit at the dining table. There are 2 girls from Australia already eating. They also visited northern Sri Lanka, Polonnaruwa and Sigiriya in Dambulla. Contrary to us, they were able to visit the ruins in Polonnaruwa and they really enjoyed it.

For dinner we have a nice selection of curries with rice. There is a potato curry, dal, green beans and chicken. It is absolutely delicious, the best I've had in Sri Lanka. The food is not very hot though, just warmish. Always been this way since we're in this country. At least this time, it's delicious. This meal makes me very happy. This was a good Christmas Eve meal, better than anything I expected by a mile. I wish Sarah would have been part of it. But after the meal I run downstairs to tell her the good news. She is looking forward to eating tomorrow.

DAY 7: SARAH'S TAKE

We return our key to the Takeshi Inn owner, he offers to help us hail a bus to Kandy. The advantage of this is he knows the correct bus and how to make it stop for us. But he will want to get rid of us as soon as possible, so he'll plop us on the first bus. We hope that in town, at the main bus stop, there will be more seats.

Walking into town one last time on these now familiar, muddy side streets, we see lots of people waiting around the main bus stop area. We don't know where to stand and aren't even sure which bus to take. Luckily, many of them have "Kandy" written in English. They are all pretty full, so we keep waiting. After a while, I'm starting to get hungry for breakfast and we resign ourselves to stand and take whatever bus comes next.

It's pretty chaotic to get in the bus. People are struggling to get off the bus as people push to get on. We see some white people enter the second door, closer to the back of the bus. We enter with them and get some seats. I have a woman's purse pressing into my head for most of the ride and occasionally get an elbow in the face, but I am happy to sit. I always have to close my eyes and it's much easier when seated.

As we near our destination, we stop at a gated compound with manicured lawn, tall trees and old buildings bordering a large lake at the base of beautiful green mountains. Something about it makes me think of Indiana Jones; I can easily picture Dr. Jones with this building in the backdrop. (Postscript fact check: One of Indiana Jones movies was actually shot in Kandy!) This is the cinematic Sri Lanka I adore. Lots of white tourists get off here and I want to be one of them, but Cedric is too far away to get his attention. The streets of Kandy are narrow and because it has a small town feel, the amount of traffic is mind boggling. It takes us such a long time to get to the bus station that people are just hopping off the bus as we crawl in traffic. The seats are clearing and I can move beside Cedric. We hop off before the bus station because it's just taking too long. Now we are in a jam of people trying to cross a tiny road overrun by cars. There's a lot of honking and it smells like exhaust. People and their umbrellas take up every square inch of sidewalk space.

TIP 45 – When travelling to Kandy from the north by bus, get off at the Temple of the Tooth. Since it is right before Kandy's ridiculously congested city centre, it will be faster to walk from the Temple than to wait until you arrive at the bus terminal.

On our way to the mall, we pass an open market. It's busy, colourful and full of chatter. It feels good to be in a city again. There's structure, people and, more importantly, it feels like we have options. Kandy city centre is actually quite compact and we quickly reach the mall.

From low ceiling to small stores and narrow hallways, everything in this mall seems too small. A cramped version of what I'm used to. We take the escalators up to the highly anticipated food court, which is closed. It looks like it's never opened, but maybe they are on Christmas holidays...

The only place serving food is Burger King. We eat and enjoy the A/C. I gaze out the large windows and admire the view. The city is in a valley surrounded with green mountains speckled with houses in the jungle. It's lovely.

It's now late enough that we can check-in and since it's unpleasant to explore the city with heavy bags, we decide to head to the guesthouse. Stepping out of the mall, a tuk tuk stops in the middle of the road to pick us up. Cedric asks him if he knows the guesthouse and what the price is. Cedric tries to bargain, but the driver stays firm at 500 rupees. He is blocking traffic and we just want to go, so we accept.

We drive through the city and turn onto a road that climbs the mountain. On our way up the hill, we pass small stores and tiny shacks. There are small landslides and trees broken on the road.

The driver explains that it is because of all the rain. I ask him if it usually rains at this time, he says it doesn't usually rain because it should be the dry season. The road to our guesthouse is a maze, but luckily there are small signs for "Hanthana Holiday Rooms" at every turn. Since the area is called Hanthana, it is really important to pay attention to each sign and make sure the "Holiday Rooms" part is there.

The tuk tuk drops us off in the middle of a road, points down another road and tells us it's down there. They are redoing this little street, paving equipment abandoned and collecting rain. The homes are very nice up here in the mountains and our guesthouse is no exception. We are greeted by a smiling woman who welcomes us into her home. At the covered entryway, Cedric slips off his Velcro sandals and follows the woman into the home through large wooden doors propped open. I am a little slower because I have to untie my sneakers. I hurry inside to catch up, but turn back to make sure my shoes are safe from the rain. I freeze when a large greyish monkey, about as big as a medium-sized dog, enters the house. Walking on all fours, he silently glides past those large wooden doors, until he spots me and he freezes too. Then he slowly backs out of the house and by the time I reach the entryway, he has disappeared. I am so excited, but there is no one to tell. Cedric is getting the grand tour from the homeowner.

It doesn't look like much from outside, but the home is beautiful. Built into the mountain slope, the house looks out onto a forest and when the mist clears, you can see some city in the valley below. On the main floor is a large sitting room, kitchen, dining room, outdoor veranda, and other areas curtained-off that only the resident family accesses. On the lower level is another living room with couch, computer (and Wi-Fi!) and our room. We are led down a hallway where we pass a wrought iron gate leading to an outdoor, sheltered area full of piles of laundry and drying laundry. We pass two more rooms, until we arrive at ours, which has a double bed and small table. There is a shared bathroom close by (with a real shower stall). The toilet and shower are dated, but scrubbed spotlessly clean. No soap scum in the shower, no hair in the drain and tiles are gleaming. Our room is in the same state. All our previous rooms have been so grubby that I really notice and appreciate this effort.

The host offers us tea, so we drop our bags and take it upstairs in the living room. The furniture is very nice. Again, everything is spotless. A lively dog prances toward us. Black, shorthair, muscular with stubby legs and tail. Yay! He is excited to see us and wiggles underneath our seated legs to settle at our feet. He looks up at us and I see his tan muzzle and chest, his eyes are smaller than I expected. Some kind of dachshund. We pet him and he is content to enjoy our attention. The bond lasts about 10 minutes before he hears something and starts barking and making a ruckus. I am disappointed to lose the highlight of my trip so soon.

We finish our tea and I check out the balcony. All I can see is tall trees and mist; this is living in the clouds. We are so happy with this accommodation, our best yet.

We sit in the basement living room where Wi-Fi reception is great. The beauty of Kandy makes me want to write in this diary and gets me motivated to answer emails, upload our pictures and leave some reviews on TripAdvisor of where we've been so far.

Dinner at the guesthouse costs about 500 rupees per person. I don't eat supper with everyone because I'm not feeling that well from Burger King. Cedric goes upstairs to eat and says it's delicious; the best meal he's had in Sri Lanka. I am slightly disappointed that I didn't join but still not feeling great, so it probably wouldn't have been worth the money. It's quite cool in the room, but at least they've given us a spare blanket.

DAY 8: DECEMBER 25, 2014

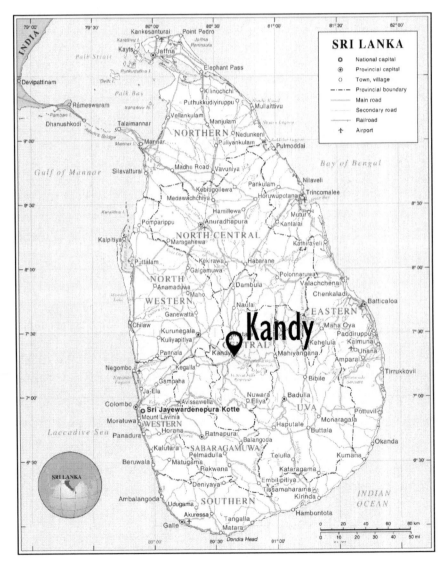

It's Christmas morning and I have a Skype call scheduled with my mom. I get up and go in the living room to make the call, but the owners are serving breakfast and Sarah is hungry, so we go upstairs and sit at the kitchen table. The owner wishes us a "Happy Christmas" and we are served an omelette with toast. The toasts are freshly toasted! For the first time in this country, we will be eating fresh toasts this morning. A little later on, the owner gets out a beautiful Christmas log cake! Amazing and a very nice way to start the day.

After breakfast, we head downstairs to call my mom. We have a long chat with all my step-cousins. They are acting all crazy, they almost seem to be drunk. Turns out they actually are. My mom tells us they ate some chocolates with alcohol in them. We then chat with my bro and he tells us about his experience in India, which is quite similar to our experience in Sri Lanka. After our Skype chat, the owner calls us a tuk tuk to go into town. Kandy is a beautiful city, so we decide to just go downtown and walk around. Unfortunately, the traffic congestion makes it highly polluted with most cars coughing out black smoke from their exhaust. It's actually kind of unpleasant.

The city itself is very old and very busy with cars and pedestrians. Everyone is walking around with their open umbrellas and it's hard to get through the crowds.

What makes this city beautiful is its surroundings. It's stunning. The city is surrounded with mountains full of jungle and houses. Never seen anything like it. Kandy is also home to a popular tourist attraction: Temple of the Tooth of Buddha. This place allegedly houses one of Buddha's teeth. But you don't actually get to see the famous tooth. All you see is a box, which supposedly contains said tooth. The entrance fee for this "attraction" is quite high at 1,500 rupees, to simply wait in line for 30-60 minutes and walk in front of the box containing the tooth and gaze at it for a few seconds before the line moves on. Again, we decide to avoid the tourist trap.

Instead we walk around the temple then go to a nearby café that I found on TripAdvisor. It's got good reviews, so we hope it will be good. The café is really nice, it is an old style, located in what used to be a hotel. I order a vegetarian wrap and Sarah orders tea. The food is alright but not great. Sarah has a chat with her aunt while I eat.

After our meal, we walk around some more and go to another café, once again highly rated on TripAdvisor. Sarah has a coffee and I order 2 of their grilled sandwiches, one ham and cheese and the other more dessert-like, banana and chocolate. While we wait for our order, a young lady has an emotional Skype call with her family. She is yelling Spanish into her computer. With no headphones we hear her family yelling back through the computer's speakers. It's Christmas, so we understand. 30 minutes later when her call is done, she apologizes to us for being so loud. Nice of her to at least acknowledge that she was annoying. Our grilled sandwiches are served and we devour them quickly, they are delicious.

We had a very nice day in Kandy, one of the nicest yet in this country. We go back to the hotel in time for dinner.

Dinner is served, once again, at 8 pm. This time, Sarah joins me and we are also joined by a French family; husband and wife, and two kids. Sarah agrees this is the best Sri Lankan food we've had since we're here, even though the food is once again, barely warm. At least it's delicious and we are very happy to be at a very, very comfortable place for Christmas. This is the most comfortable we've been so far, by far. After dinner we go downstairs to have a Skype call with Sarah's dad and step-mom. It's been our best day so far in this country. We feel blessed. Did I mention it's raining?

DAY 8: SARAH'S TAKE

Breakfast is nice. Two Australian girls at the table talk about their Sri Lanka experience and I tune out as soon as someone mentions there are actually *two dogs* in this house, a mom and son! They look identical, except the mom is a bit smaller and more delicate. After breakfast and Skyping with Cedric's family, we head down to the city. The owner calls a tuk tuk for us and it costs 300 rupees. That's 40% less than what we paid yesterday…but who's counting?

The rain is just spitting today, so I can see through the jungle out to the valley below. Everywhere is green and it's just beautiful. Coming from North America, where we bulldoze our environment to start level and clean, it's remarkable to see so much nature in an urban setting. This "green" isn't the nice line of evenly spaced trees down a suburban boulevard; it's raw jungle foliage.

Despite the winding roads and two-storey homes carved into its cliffs, there is no controlling these mountains. As the landslides will attest. Waiting for the tuk tuk to arrive, I see two monkeys quietly strolling on the neighbour's roof. I do love this city.

I ask the driver to drop us off at the Temple of the Tooth, my imaginary setting for Indiana Jones. It's crawling with visitors coming and going. I have no plans of going inside. Like a kid who would rather play with the packaging than the toy, I'm happy to admire the architecture and grounds.

With the right budget, it would be good fun to be part of the crowd.

The architecture inside is supposed to be lovely. But another $40 activity? No, thank you. So we walk along the adjoining lake and take a closer look at the Temple. Lots of Sri Lankans are wearing white clothing (light colours to show respect).

After we've had our fill of gazing through the gated fence, we head to the Empire Hotel café for tea. It's over 100 years old and while its old architecture has been preserved, inside it has been stylized.

The walls are dusty rose with white wainscoting and teal accents. The furniture is a mix of dark brown, heavy wooden pieces and white rattan. We are seated in the rattan armchairs, with a round seat and chair back that is threaded and flared out to look like a peacock's tail. It reminds me of Alice in Wonderland and so I have to have a spot of loose leaf tea at 230 rupees and Cedric orders the Royal Lankan wrap at 590 rupees. Plus tax and service charge, it comes to 900 rupees. The wrap is homemade and stuffed with parippu vada (think Indian falafel), comes with a side of taro chips and coleslaw. It's a bit loud in the restaurant, but I take a call from my aunt and it feels nice to chat with family.

We walk around the city centre and realize just how compact it is. Down one street, you can find a shops selling luggage next to one selling Tupperware, fresh produce or dried fish. I buy socks at 100 rupees a pair from a man at a folding table on a busy street corner. Then I pop into a clothing store advertising a Christmas sale. It's packed, but I manage to find some "granny panties" at 60 rupees each.

TIP 46 – If you have anything to buy (clothes, food, equipment) or require any service (bank, cell plan) make sure you take care of it in the bigger cities (Colombo, Kandy). Once you get more into the country, you lose options.

Feeling good about having some fresh garments, we head to Natural Coffee, a café overlooking the Tooth Temple grounds. It's right next to the Empire Hotel café. We order off the promotional menu and get some sort of deal. I get an espresso shake with banana, milk and sugar. Cedric orders us a ham, tomato & cheese grilled sandwich and banana & chocolate grilled sandwich. It's all very rich and delicious.

Next we decide to buy some alcohol to have with Christmas dinner tonight. Cargills Food City has its liquor store inside the grocery store. From the other cities we've visited, it is usually a small counter, kind of like a pharmacy. We see a sign outside that because of the holiday, alcohol will not be sold on December 25th. Darn.

It's been a nice day, but we decide to head back to the guesthouse. The tuk tuk wants to charge us 500 again, but Cedric gets him down to 350 (400 with tip).

I am eager to try on my socks. They have absolutely no stretch and while I can stuff my feet into them, I can't walk in them. Ha ha! I guess 300 a pair was a better deal than 300 for 3 pairs that I will toss. At least the woolen pair that Cedric bought from the man on the street are good. Like all of our clothes, his sandals are permanently damp and the socks will make him more comfortable.

We eat supper at the guesthouse. Curry is on the menu tonight. We have spicy mango, chicken and pumpkin curries, dal and curried haricot vert. Served with steamed white rice. A lot of the rice we've eaten in Sri Lanka is a shorter and wider oval than the long grain rice I'm used to.

TIP 47 – Curry leaves are edible, but most people push them to the side of their plate. I (Sarah) like to take a small mouthful of food, pick up a leaf, bite down (still intact) to release the amazing aroma, and then push the leaf to the side of my plate. There is no substitute for fresh curry leaves and unless you know someone who is growing a curry tree in in their backyard, this is the only part of the world where you can enjoy the unique aroma.

To my delight, the house cat comes to sit at the table with us. Not on the table, just very politely on a kitchen chair. Eventually, a French family replaces the cat and we have a nice chat with them about their visit in the country.

We ask the host about our trip tomorrow and he tells us all trains are cancelled due to the landslides. He doesn't know when the tracks will be cleared or when they will reopen the train. We ask about bus. He tells us about an A/C bus to our next destination. He sells it well and we are excited about this possible VIP transportation. He guarantees that his driver can reserve seats for us at the front of the bus. Soon enough it's time to call my dad on Skype. We have a great Christmas chat with the folks back home and we finish our evening leaving some TripAdvisor reviews of the guesthouses and restaurants we've used this past week and writing about our Sri Lanka experience. The cute dogs come to visit us and accept out petting as we write in the lower level sitting room. I love this place!

DAY 9: DECEMBER 26, 2014

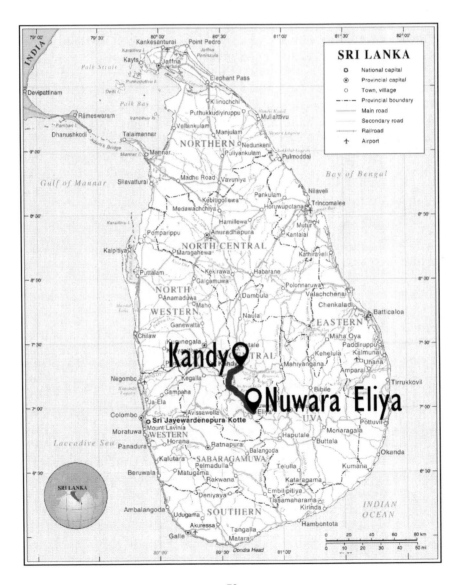

We now feel re-energized. We hope our time in Kandy symbolizes a new start on our journey. We are kind of sad to leave this place. But at the same time, it's good to keep moving forward. We get up and have a delicious breakfast and are on our way. Today we're heading for Nuwara Eliya. The owner arranges our tuk tuk ride and tells us we'll get front row seat in an A/C bus. This sounds great and we're looking forward to it.

The tuk tuk drives us to the bus station. Once there, he stops at the bus station entrance and points and says, "This one."

We are about 200 meters away from 15 buses, so it's quite hard to know which one he is pointing at. So we ask, "Which one?"

He seems annoyed and drives into the bus station, right next to the correct bus. We pay him and he leaves. The "A/C" bus is not quite what I imagined. I was expecting a modern coach bus. I guess I was expecting too much from this country. The bus is quite small and just as uncomfortable as the regular buses. Worse, actually, because the aisle seats pull out so that even the alley is filled with seats. You feel even more squished. Sarah and I are not sitting together, but at least we have a seat, so at least that's good.

TIP 48 – Forget the A/C bus. If it is busy, you will be so squished that you won't feel any A/C, only body heat. Because it's a smaller vehicle, you feel more road bumps too.

Nuwara Eliya is the highest city in the country, at an elevation of almost 2 km above sea level. The trip to Nuwara Eliya takes around 2 hours. It's not very far, but the mountain S-shape roads and landslide cleanup slows us down. Workers try to clear the mess. Fallen trees and power lines narrow the road to one lane. Houses teeter on the edge.

For the most part, the view is spectacular with green farms on green mountains and trickling streams feeding rushing rivers. I take a lot of videos of the flashing landscape because it's just too nice.

When we arrive in Nuwara Eliya, Sarah gets out of the bus trembling and confused. She keeps asking me where we are. Concerned, I ask her if she needs a doctor. A tuk tuk driver approaches and seeing that Sarah is leaning up against the wall, has tears rolling down her face and doesn't look well, he offers to drive us to a hospital. Sarah denies politely once. When he insists, she turns to me, holds her sweater up to block the driver and says, "Get this f**k the f**k away from me." Whoa.

She refuses to tell me what is happening, so I have no idea what to do. We go sit in the bus station for a while. After 10-15 minutes she says, "I'm not feeling well from the bus, let's go to the hotel." I ask her if she wants to walk or take a tuk tuk. She says walking is better. The hotel is not too far out of town, only 15-minute walk.

On the way there, I stop at the store for our train tickets to our next destination. Sarah waits outside. I go in and asks if I can get our train tickets printed. The clerk picks up the phone and calls the Rajadhani office. She speaks on the phone for a couple of minutes and then passes it to me. I cannot understand a single thing the lady on the phone is saying. Sounds English, I think, but I don't understand anything. I ask her to repeat 3 times and then I just have to hang up on her. The lady at the counter, seeing that I didn't understand anything, tells me I have to go to Mobitel at the train station... We leave the ticket office and head to the hotel.

Sarah is sick and not in a good mood. I have my phone with Google maps open, but there are not many street signs and not many addresses, so it makes it much more difficult to find our way. Even the local tuk tuks don't know where anything is half the time! I have to orient myself with the shape of the streets and landmarks. I am happy to say that we make it to the guesthouse in one try.

At the guesthouse, Sarah gets a ginger tea, which turns out to be delicious, made from real ginger chunks. The host shows us to our room. Since Sarah is not feeling well, he tells her to let him know if there anything he can do. He also mentions that his sister is a doctor; he can call her and she will be here within minutes. We kindly decline his offer, but we are quite cold so we ask for a heater. He says we don't need it, but he will bring an extra blanket.

Nuwara Eliya is quite cold, and did I mention it's raining? Being very high in the mountains, the temperature today afternoon is 14 degrees Celsius. At night, it gets to 11. This might not sound that cold, but these homes are not designed for it. There's no heater in the room and we don't have a jacket. Thankfully, the host gave us a lot of blankets, so I think we can sit comfortably in the room (on the bed, of course, nowhere else to sit).

So far I find the host a little intense. Even though he is very nice in trying to care for Sarah, he is boastful about his TripAdvisor reviews and how everybody who comes here love the food. It puts me off and I guess we'll see for ourselves at dinner.

At 7:30 pm, dinner is served. Seems common that people eat late in this country. The host, JP, tells us that his wife, Loga, has made a special soup for Sarah. We are actually both touched by this attention. JP tells us he's been worrying about Sarah all afternoon and he had to do something, so he had his wife make the special soup. I get to have a bowl too and it is absolutely delicious. Next up, a chicken curry with a thin bread that looks like a pancake. We dig in and as much as I didn't like JP bragging about his food, I have to admit he was absolutely right. The best food we've had in Sri Lanka, even better than the last place. Loga is cooking the food in front of our eyes, and serving the chapatti as soon as it's ready, out of the pan, which means the food is hot. This is the first time in Sri Lanka that we have piping hot food.

Sarah is sick, it's raining, it's cold, we're tired, but JP and Loga are helping alleviating all the negatives. I really like JP and Loga. We feel very well taken care of, like family. We go to bed and I sleep like a rock. The pile of blankets keep us warm.

TIP 49 – Don't be shy to ask for more blankets if you need them. The hosts usually have plenty of extra.

DAY 9: SARAH'S TAKE

We pack up for Nuwara Eliya and go eat breakfast. There is a new family at the kitchen table, Sri Lankans that have come from Colombo to Kandy for the holidays. They each take two slices of toast, spread them with margarine and eat it like a sandwich. Then when their egg arrives, they have another two pieces of toast with the egg. Is this why we are offered so much toast at breakfast? I rush through breakfast to make a Christmas Skype call to my family.

The host calls the tuk tuk and we go wait at the end of the driveway for our ride. It's another beautiful day in the trees and the mist. The host comes jogging over to us because we forgot to pay our bill for the dinners we ate. Oops. He proudly talks about his son who studied at university in America and now works there. I realize this family is even wealthier than I thought because American universities are expensive. He is still there chatting with us when the driver arrives. As we climb into the tuk tuk, there is a heated discussion between the driver and the host. It sounds quite angry and I've heard enough Sinhalese now to know this isn't just "the way they talk." I finally draw back the tuk tuk curtain to look at our host, his scowl disappears and he smile brightly at me, "Ok, he will take you to the AC bus." But continues yelling at the driver once I let the curtain fall back down.

Whether from the argument or his general disposition, our tuk tuk driver seems grumpy. He's honking and gesturing at every vehicle he races past. This is normal in a city, but we are on deserted mountain roads. I find his road rage a bit dangerous given the slippery roads and landslides, so I ask him some personal questions. "Do you celebrate Christmas…Is this much rain normal…" Just something to bring him out of his funk. It kind of works and he softens up a little bit.

The highly anticipated A/C bus is a letdown. Compared to the tall school buses we've taken previously, it's quite a short, little bus. It's already full. Forget seats at the front, we don't even sit together and get some of the last seats remaining. The driver places Cedric at a window seat next to an older white gentleman. Because the seats are so tiny and you are glued to your seatmate, they are "courteous" about seating women with women. I am seated next to a Sri Lankan woman who is already taking up some of my seat.

The man next to Cedric makes a show of checking the window seat before Cedric sits down. I figure he is looking for something he dropped. I try to Skype my family using the cell phone, but can't figure out how to logout of Cedric's account. I pass it to Cedric seated in front of me and ask him how to do it. The man next to Cedric sees we are together and offers me his seat on the condition that my seat has a working seatbelt. After inspection, he loudly explains with a German accent, "Sorry, but the lady is too large. Since I am not so small myself, I cannot trade seats." I am a bit embarrassed, but hopefully she doesn't speak English, and I do appreciate that he offered.

With all the rushing around this morning, I forgot to take my Dramamine 1 hour before departure, so I pop it on the bus. Terrible mistake. After about half an hour, we are still in the city traffic, braking and accelerating with Indian music blaring out the speakers. I've had my eyes closed, but with so much jerking around, I don't feel good. I pop another pill.

An hour later and I am so nauseous. These are winding, bumpy roads in the best of times. I'm sure with all the landslides, the braking and accelerating it's probably worse than ever. I am vaguely aware that we stop occasionally, but I don't really know why. Feeling worse and worse, I wonder when the pills will kick in. I haven't thrown up in a car since I was 10. I take some pride in the fact that even without pills, I can usually control my motion sickness at a level so as not to throw up (visualising, pressure points, closing my eyes, etc.). It is inconceivable that I would be sick on this bus.

I start to feel a little drowsy and think, "Finally, the pills are kicking in! Relief is coming." But the nausea doesn't go away. In fact, I stop feeling any of the A/C that we paid triple the price for and just feel the body heat radiating from the two people I am sandwiched between. I am hot and sweating. Removing some layers, I feel cooler instantly and it gives me temporary relief.

My backpack is on my lap and making me retain heat. I crack open my eyes and lower the bag to my feet. Another mistake. Somewhere in the 3 seconds it took me to open my eyes and move my bag to the floor, I am hit with a wall of nausea that makes my sinuses hurt. I quickly squeeze my eyes shut and think cool thoughts. Cold walks in the forest, fresh air, snow. Getting rid of the bag and my layers has cooled me some. I tell myself the nausea will pass as long as I stick to the plan: eyes closed, pressure points, visualisation, breathing through the mouth (have I mentioned that the man next to me smells like onions and curry?). But with every twist and turn and bump in the road, it only gets worse.

I feel my stomach start to rise, so I lift up my chin and the nausea doesn't rise quite so powerfully. I raise my chin until I cannot go any further. I sit up as straight as I can, trying to get higher than my stomach. As I get taller, I start to feel a draft of air. Someone has opened a window! Thank you, thank you. I feel relief from the building nausea as the evaporating sweat cools my skin. Sadly it only lasts a little while, and soon the nausea builds again.

I start to feel a prickly numbness in my hands and then my feet. They must be falling asleep, although I've never had limbs fall asleep within seconds like this. The numbness gets more intense and becomes a kind of buzzing electricity in my hands and feet. I know shaking, trembling muscles and this is not it. Pressure builds in my extremities. It's like they are swelling and my skin is too tight, but at the same time, they start to feel weightless. I've never felt anything like this before, what the heck is going on?

It is inevitable, I am going to be sick. I lift chin up as far as it can go. I desperately want to ask Cedric for a plastic bag to be sick in, but I know that as soon as I open my mouth, I will throw up. I know there's a plastic bag in my backpack, but where? I can't open my eyes and look because that's what got me into this downward spiral of nausea in the first place.

It's so packed on this bus, I don't know what will happen if I'm sick. I will make a mess of my bag and everyone else's stuff around me. Maybe other people will be sick at the sight of it and throw up too. Will they stop the bus and make us get off? I shouldn't be thinking like this, my visualisation is off. I can't hold my wrists because my hands are numb and vibrating with some weird swelling electricity. My chin is as high as my spine will allow and—my stomach does a mini lurch. Phew; dry heave, no solids.

Another spasm and I retch into my mouth, but before I can swallow it down, my stomach heaves again. This time part of my breakfast comes up and my cheeks swell out. I think of eggs, toast and black coffee as I force this disgusting bolus back down my throat. I retch and swallow one more time, grateful that I'm not making a mess on the bus. My hands and feet are tingle-buzzing like crazy. But for the first time my nausea is actually decreasing and I feel some relief. Suddenly aware that I'm leaning forward, sweating profusely with closed eyes and an upturned face contorted in pain, I wonder if anyone heard my heaving.

Then the bus slows to a crawl. I don't know why we've slowed: landslide, canteen or bathroom break, collect more passengers. I hear rustling and open my eyes to see people getting off. Can we get off here too? When I feel I can speak without projectile vomiting, I hit Cedric on shoulder, "Where?" He looks at me puzzled. I repeat, "Where?" No time to explain, I've opened my eyes too long and the numbness in my hands and feet starts building that humming electricity. Again, I feel the distended weightlessness in my limbs and know what comes next. Cedric gets up with his bag. My arms and legs are trembling and I can barely lift my bag, but I want to exit this bus at all costs.

Outside, it's loud and smells like exhaust. I walk over to a wall and lean on it. Cedric finds me trembling and teary-eyed. "What's going on?"

I can't string a sentence together. I ask Cedric, "Where are we?"

He replies, "At the bus station."

"What city?"

Cedric says we've arrived. A tuk tuk comes over, "Do you need hospital?"

Go away, go away. I sit in the bus station for a while. I can't talk. I could throw up at any moment. We walk to the hotel, it's so cold that people are wearing woolen caps and winter jackets, but I'm in my tank top, sweating.

We arrive at the Nidwalden Resort. Our host, JP, asks if we want tea, I request ginger tea. He orders the young woman ironing towels to go make it. He's tells us that they have great reviews, his wife's cooking. I want to be polite, but I'm not really following, to be honest; I just need to rest. He asks what we want to do next, I say I'm unwell from the trip, it's my stomach and I just want to rest. He says to go rest and we'll eat supper later. He tells us maybe the trains will be back up in couple of days. We are hopeful for our train ride to our next destination.

The room is on the second floor. It's good. Basic, but has a private bathroom. It's so cold. JP gets me an extra blanket. I am so cold, but eventually fall asleep. JP comes to check on us later, and I say that I don't want supper. Same old story. I feel like crap, don't really trust the food and want to save money. But he insist it will be better if I eat and that they will make me a light meal. I give in and Cedric is happy because he hates it when I want to skip meals.

We go down for dinner and sit at a long wooden table in the warmest room in the house. We are introduced to Loga, JP's wife. With a Bindi on her forehead, Loga is not like the other Sri Lankans we've met. She is at the table watching a dubbed Indian soap opera playing on the small TV in the corner. They quiz me on my state. I say I'm feeling much better after my rest. Loga gets up and starts working in the kitchen to the side of room. JP tells me they were quite worried about me. He thought I might have eaten some bad food and they wanted to call a doctor. He tells me that they made tonight's meal especially for me with lots of ginger and garlic, which will help my stomach. This embarrasses me because I don't like strangers fussing over me. We are the only guests at the table. JP offers Cedric a beer and says I can have two bowls of soup since I am not having beer. We are served the vegetable soup and it is so, so good. Lentil, potato, onion, garlic, ginger spices and fresh coriander leaves. I'm not even hungry, but I happily overstuff myself. Tastes homemade and not salty. Just delicious.

We tell them as much and JP says, "Loga makes food the old way, like the mother or grandmother way." We see Loga rolling out dough, she tells us it is chapatti. They bring it to the table hot and fresh, simply amazing. While we devour the dry spiced chicken and dal, JP explains the difference between naan, roti and chapatti. Something about the flour, I'm not really listening because this is the best meal I've had in over a week and just keep shoveling it into my mouth. Loga asks if it is too spicy. Cedric says that it's perfect (which it is). She laughs, "That's what everyone says: perfect."

We inhale two portions, stuffing the dal and chicken in the chapatti fajita-style since we don't know the Sri Lankan way of eating with our hands. During our meal, JP gets a cancellation call and tells us people are afraid to drive here because of the landslides. I wonder if we should have been more cautious and cancelled this leg of our trip too. JP tells us that during the war, when there were no tourists, they were potato farmers.

Since the soap opera on TV is of Indian origin, I ask about languages. Loga explains that there are two languages in Sri Lanka, Sinhalese and Tamil. They are Tamil, but they also speak Sinhalese.

It usually takes me a long time to feel comfortable around new people, but they are so genuinely kind that by the time supper is finished, I feel at home. We go to bed full, warm and cared for. I finally feel good enough to tell Cedric about my experience on this morning's A/C bus ride. He can't understand why I waited all day to tell him. He's shocked while he was happily filing the beautiful vistas, I was in so much pain not 3 feet away. It's always odd when someone right next to you, doing exactly what you are doing, has a completely different experience. Perhaps it's what life is like for the Tamil in this country. They are living and working side by side with the Sinhalese, but their experience has been more challenging.

DAY 10: DECEMBER 27, 2014

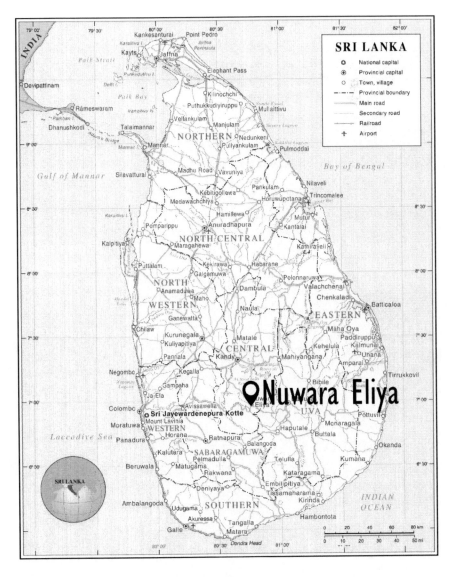

This morning we got up at around 8 am and went downstairs right away to get breakfast. We are served coffee and tea. It's much warmer in the kitchen with the elements on and with the hot tea, it feels good to warm up. I check the weather on my smartphone; it's 12 degrees Celsius in Nuwara Eliya.

This morning we are having a Sri Lankan breakfast. I must admit I am a bit wary as I've seen others have it and it didn't look that appetizing. But I am hopeful as dinner was absolutely delicious.

JP starts by bringing us little pieces of roti (flat bread) along with coconut sambal. It consists of shredded coconut, lime, garlic and red chillies. It looks good. JP shows us how to eat it. You take a spoon, put some sambal on the little piece of roti and eat it. It's delicious. We finish the 6 little pieces of roti in a couple of minutes.

Almost as soon as we are done, he brings us a whole piece of roti along with potato curry and dal. He then shows us the Sri Lankan way of eating, i.e. with your hand. You tear a piece of roti and use the bread as the utensil. You can drag your bread on your plate and grab a little bit of everything, a little bit like an excavator. Again, the potato curry and the dal is absolutely delicious. The best we've had in this country, by far.

TIP 50 – Eating the Sri Lankan way:
i.   **Wash your hands**
ii. **Use your right hand only (one hand will feel awkward, especially tearing bread)**
iii. **Tear bread or grab a chunk of rice**
iv. **Mix up your rice/curry/sambal/etc.**
v.   **Pinch food with your fingertips (if you are using bread, cover food with bread and pinch a little food inside)**
Supposedly, you shouldn't get sauce up higher than your first joint, so really use the tips of your fingers.

As Sarah and I devour our meal, Loga has trouble keeping up cooking more roti. But she does catch up and bring more and more roti and dal and potato curry, until we have to tell them to stop. We are incredibly full. This meal is very good for our spirits. We are now looking forward to our day.

JP tells us we can go visit a tea factory, it's only 30 minutes by bus. Sarah is still recovering from yesterday's bus ride, so another one is out of the question. Instead, we decide to go walk around town. I saw on TripAdvisor there is supposed to be a very nice-looking park, Victoria Park, in the center of town, so we put our warm clothes on and head towards the park, it's only a 15-minute walk.

Nuwara Eliya is a really nice-looking town. There are large brick sidewalks and police officers at every corner of every street. We learn that the police presence is due to the President coming to town tomorrow for the political campaign.

As we arrive at the park entrance, we find out there is a fee to enter the park. Duh! Of course there is a fee. Absolutely nothing is free in this country. The fee for tourists is 300 rupees per person. The fee for locals in 20 rupees per person, a 1500% markup. From the entrance, it seems like a nice-looking park, but nothing special, maybe as nice as Central Park in Manhattan. Anyways, we decide we have nothing else to do today and 300 rupees won't break the bank, so we pay and get in.

The park is nice indeed. For Sri Lanka, this is actually very well-maintained, nothing like the rest of the country. We walk around the park for around an hour and that's enough time to go around the entire park and return to the entrance.

We're cold and wet (it's raining, obviously), so I check on TripAdvisor for a café where we can warm up. I find one that is actually only a 10-minute walk, it's called Grand Hotel Café. The café is a very nice, cozy and relaxing place to warm up and just relax with a hot beverage. We stay there for lunch. Sarah doesn't eat because she doesn't trust the cold deviled chicken salad. They make quite a few "deviled" foods (chips, etc.) and, like the name suggests, it's spicy. After several hours at the café, we decide to walk back to our cold hotel, not really looking forward to it, but at least looking forward to what is probably going to be, a delicious dinner.

Once we arrive at the hotel JP is there to welcome us and asks us what we did today. We tell him that we couldn't go to the tea plantation, but we'll have another chance to visit a tea plantation at our next destination, Ella. JP announces that he has some bad news for us. He and his wife were invited out for dinner, so they will not be able to cook dinner for us. He offers to interrupt his dinner and bring us food from a good restaurant at around 7:30 pm. Now, after tasting Loga's food, it's highly disappointing. Bad news not over, JP tells us that due to the landslides, all trains have been cancelled. We will have to take the bus to our next destination. We already bought our train tickets and they are not refundable. It's not very much money, so it's not the end of the world. What is highly unfortunate, is to have to take the bus again, which is highly uncomfortable and gets Sarah sick. Because we are in a small town, we probably won't get a seat either as the buses are already full coming from the big city of Kandy. JP assures us that he will call his good friend and tuk tuk driver, who will reserve seats for us.

JP continues and says that we are currently the only guests at the hotel, all the other travelers having cancelled their stay due to the landslides, but that a family is due to arrive later tonight and he asks if we could answer the door when they ring. We say no problem.

We hang out in the living room watching satellite TV and writing until we hear a car coming. It's around 7:30 pm so it could either be JP or the family. Turns out, it's the family. They are from Hong Kong and have one kid, along with their driver. It doesn't take long before we start conversing about our experience in this country. They are expressing the same frustrations as we've been having so far in Sri Lanka. It feels good to meet other people who share the same experiences. They ramble away and whine about how this country is disorganized, people are unfriendly, everything is outrageously expensive, etc. Everything we've been thinking as well. It feels good to hear that we're not the only ones. We're not crazy; it's a relief.

It's 8 pm and we see a car coming in the driveway, it's JP with our food! We are starving. The food is good but not nearly as good as Loga's. Once we're done, we go back to the living room and watch Night at the Museum 2 with the family. We go to bed and are not eager for tomorrow. It's going to be a long travel day. Did I mention it's raining?

In fact, it almost hasn't stopped raining since we stepped foot in this country. Granted it's rainy season in the north, but it's not rainy season in Negombo, Colombo, Kandy and Nuwara Eliya, where it hasn't stopped raining since we arrived in Sri Lanka. Our clothes are permanently damp. We stink, literally, and there is nothing we can do about it. Most guesthouses we stayed at offer laundry service, but none of them have dryers. They just air dry their laundry outside. However, because of the non-stop rain, they are having trouble drying their own stuff. Humidity levels are almost always at 100%. Nothing dries in these conditions. We saw JP's staff actually have to iron all the sheets to dry them completely, otherwise they remain damp.

DAY 10: SARAH'S TAKE

Breakfast is superb: fresh roti (thicker flatbread made with whole wheat flour), dal, potato curry, coconut sambal (a spicy, zesty, salty delight). So, so, so good. I accept a fried egg served with lots of pepper, Cedric doesn't. Feeling much better today and looking forward to our walk into town, I put on all my shirts (7 layers).

Our guesthouse is at the outer edge of town, at the base of a mountain. On our way into town, I see the small fields near JP's home. Small patches of carrots, potatoes and other crops I can't identify on the terraced farms. It is all green and misty grey with the occasional pop of red soil peeking through.

There is an unusual combination of hardy conifer and cedar (cypress) trees alongside the more tropical ferns and fruit-bearing, flowering trees. We don't often see pines growing next to palms. The town is small and we quickly reach the number one tourist attraction of Nuwara Eliya, the golf course. Everywhere is incredibly scenic, with stately views and far off waterfalls in the misty mountains. I imagine it must be even more amazing on a clear day.

TIP 51 – Definitely walk everywhere in Nuwara Eliya, if you can. It's a small town and you miss much of the charm if you drive around.

Victoria Park is lovely and has a trimmed, English garden feel. We walk by a rose garden, which would be glorious in flowering season. Obviously, there is not much blooming in late December, but the park is enjoyable nonetheless.

TIP 52 – Flowering season in Nuwara Eliya is April to May and August to September. Victoria Park will be most beautiful around these times.

We head to a café and warm up. A stray dog nonchalantly follows us on our walk, trotting along, pretending to ignore us, but discreetly eyeing us when he stops to sniff. It isn't until I see the dog walk up to a tree that I notice how large their trunks are. Not the enormous firs of Canada's west coast but still big. After warming up at the café, we have to head back to our chilly hotel room. Along the way, some newer constructions look like little English cottages.

We walk back to the hotel along a road that is closed to cars. Little flags are strung between the lampposts and gives the street a party atmosphere. We approach a stage in construction at the end of the street and figure it is for the President's visit. There is an election in January.

JP comes to get us in our room at 6:30 pm. He says they are leaving and we should come downstairs now. Huh? Yes, we agreed to let the new guests in, but I don't remember agreeing to wait downstairs all night...I go with the flow and we head downstairs. Loga is dressed up in a beautiful sari. With a bit of midriff and back exposed, I can't help but wonder how she is not cold. They leave and it's nice to have the place to ourselves. We turn on the TV and I keep writing.

The new guests arrive: German man, Chinese lady and little boy. Their driver is a young Sri Lankan fellow, who immediately asks if JP is here. They are all a bit put off that the hosts are not there to greet them. I ignore their discomfort and cheerfully show the family to their room, right next to ours on the second floor. Then I come downstairs to see the driver looking lost. There is no more room upstairs, so I walk him down the hallway toward the kitchen. I ask him if he's eaten because JP will be here soon with food. He says he already ate, but seems delighted to have someone paying attention to him. I drop him off in a room where a light has been left on, assuming it was made up for him. He is very nice and looks disappointed when I turn to leave. I tell him that he should come join us in the living room. It seems like he wants to, but he declines.

TIP 53 – You can opt to hire a private driver for your trip. Although you miss out on a huge part of the Sri Lankan experience by doing this, it is massively more comfortable than the buses, trains and tuk tuks that the masses use. For me (Sarah), my hesitation is not that we would have to pay for all the driver's food and accommodations, it's that they would be with us <u>all the time</u>. Sharing my holidays with a stranger would drive me absolutely mental.

We hang out with the family in the living room and get along very well with them. It turns out to be a nice evening. The woman tells us that she actually visited JP's house this morning and hated it. She told JP it was totally unacceptable and left.

I enjoy direct people, but I work to control my face so that my eyebrows don't raise at her revelation. It's no mansion, but it's certainly not a mud hut. There's carpet in each room, flush toilet and hot water tank…I guess she hasn't stayed in many Sri Lankan guesthouses.

JP is such a proud man, I can only imagine how he took the criticism. I was put off by JP's boasting at first, but I have come to see it as the way he focuses on the positive. I've only been in Sri Lanka 10 days and can't wait to leave; JP doesn't have that option. From modest potato farmers to well-rated guesthouse owners, I think his pride is justified. After all, his wife's food really *is* the best.

So, this Hong Kong family spent all day looking for something better, but everything else was booked and they came back here. We commiserate about certain aspects of Sri Lanka (as spoiled, white tourists do). Since they are doing our trip in reverse, we look at their photos of sites we have yet to see.

TIP 54 – If you are chatting with tourists that have already gone to your upcoming destinations, get their opinion on activities, restaurants, etc. in that town. As they are some of the few people in the country not trying to relieve you of your money, their opinion is truly valuable.

JP returns with our food and the atmosphere shifts. JP is polite, but guarded around the family. I am so hungry, but kind of disappointed to go eat because I really enjoy chatting with these new guests. It's been so nice to share our experience and complain without worrying about offending a local.

JP informs us that we should be at the bus station by 9:30 am. Because of the President's visit, the bus station will be closed and buses will be parked somewhere else. He says not to worry because his driver will be out early looking for where the buses will be parked. He says his driver will make sure we find the right bus and get on it. We say we'll get up and eat breakfast between around 8 am to make sure we have enough time.

The fried noodles are pretty good, but we are depressed about missing a Loga meal. As I wash our dishes, I take a look at the humble kitchen that produces such wonderful food: 4-burner range, two-burner portable, food processor, mortar and pestle, cutting board. Somehow these tools make amazing meals. Cedric and I speculate on why Loga's food is so good. Maybe because she is Tamil, her grandmother or mother brought the recipes from India when they came to work on the tea plantations, and her food has more of an Indian influence, which is why we like it so much. I put the leftovers in the fridge and spot a covered bowl of dough. Fingers crossed that fresh bread will be on the menu tomorrow!

DAY 11: DECEMBER 28, 2014

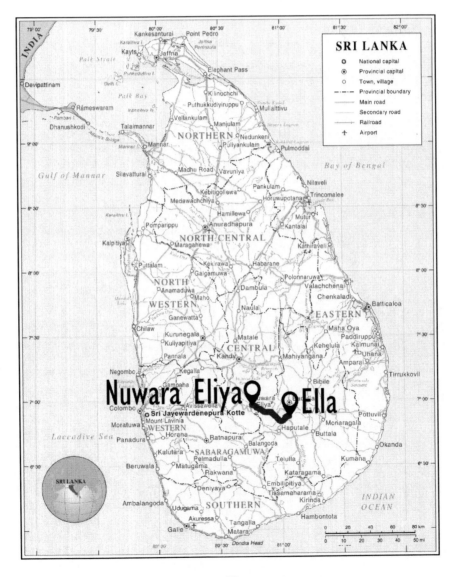

We are absolutely not looking forward to today. We're freezing cold, we stink, and we're tired. The only positive is that our next destination is around 1 km above sea level (Nuwara Eliya is close to 2 km), so temperatures should be a bit warmer.

We go downstairs to have breakfast. The Hong Kong family is already there, but it doesn't look like they've been there long, as JP and Loga are just starting to serve breakfast. This morning we are having some sort of omelette/crêpe. Think of a crêpe but with an omelette in the middle. Again, it's very good. A little later there is a second type of crêpe being served. JP calls it the sweet one. They are crêpes rolled with some sort of sweet coconut filling. Since I have a sweet tooth, that one is a winner for me, it's delicious.

TIP 55 – The Nidwalden Resort in Nuwara Eliya is also a restaurant. So if you booked elsewhere, definitely call to see if you can eat a meal there. Loga's home cooked food is worth it.

It's around 8:45 am and JP announces to us that the tuk tuk driver is coming ASAP; there is a lot of traffic and hustle and bustle because the President is coming to town today. JP tells us the President is very bad. He says all this trouble in his small city for the campaign, it's very bad; it's all disorganised. He says he's a bad President and things are hard for them, the Tamil, in general.

The region we are in is mainly Tamil. The British brought them from India earlier in the 20th century, when they had control of the country, to work in the tea fields. The local population refused to work in the fields for the British so they had to bring thousands of Tamil from India to do the job. Today almost all tea pickers are still Tamil. The north and east of the country is also inhabited by Tamil, but those people actually came to Sri Lanka their own. They are the ones who wanted to separate during the civil war. The government of Sri Lanka defeated them by eradicating all of the rebels fighting for their independence. That's one way to end a war…

By 9 o'clock we are ready, waiting at the door. JP says the tuk tuk driver should be here any minute. Time is ticking by and the driver doesn't show up. JP had been on the phone with the tuk tuk driver and he says because of the President coming, the bus is not at its normal spot so the driver is "driving all over town" to find out where the bus is.

It's now 9:30 and there is no sign of the tuk tuk driver. There is no way we are catching the 9:30 bus. I must say, I am not in a good mood right now. The town is miniscule and we've been waiting for this tuk tuk driver for 45 minutes. JP tells us we can catch another bus going to another town, we'll just have to switch there and take another bus to Ella from there… This is not good news.

It's now 9:40 and the tuk tuk driver finally shows up. I ask JP how much the tuk tuk ride should be. Because the tuk tuk driver has been "driving all over town" to find the bus that we're now not going to catch, the fee for the tuk tuk ride is going to be higher, 250 rupees... The driver drops us off and we ask which bus to take for Ella and he points from 200 meters away in the general direction of about 5 buses. I'm really not impressed by this tuk tuk driver.

You have to understand that the bus system is really for locals, so there is nobody to help tourists. The only people who speak English are the taxi drivers. They come to us and ask our destination. "Ella? There are no buses for Ella before 11 am. Do you need taxi? 7,000 rupees."

You say, "No, I don't want taxi. Where is the bus for Ella going to be?" They show you a spot and you have to trust that it's the right spot.

Two minutes later another taxi driver comes to you and tells you completely different information, "The bus for Ella is at 10:30 am and it's going to be over there." It goes on and on... 5-6 people later, telling you different information, until you are able to corroborate and pinpoint the most likely spot and time from similar information given from half the people you talked to.

It's now 10 am and the bus, we think, will come at 10:40 am. So we sit and wait. At around 10:30 am we get up and are ready in case the bus pulls in early. Tons of buses keep pulling in and out, but there is no way to tell if it's the right bus or not. So every 2 minutes, when a bus pulls in, I or Sarah has to go and ask the bus driver if he is going to Ella.

During that time another tourist comes to us and asks where we are going. She is going to Ella too. She's also been asking around and our information matches, so that's a good thing. There are starting to be lots of other tourists in the area now. We ask where they are going and they are all going to Ella too. Every time a bus pulls in, one of us asks the bus driver where he is going. It's absolutely insane. We must have asked at least 15 buses by now. Ridiculous.

It's now 10:45 and there is no sign of the Ella bus. A tourist tells us she was offered a taxi to Ella for 7,000 rupees, but it can fit up to 6 people, so we could share it. She is with her boyfriend, so with the 4 of us it would come to 3,500 rupees per couple. More money than anticipated to go to Ella (the bus is around 200 rupees per person), but at this point the extra comfort seems worth it.

A few minutes later, the correct bus finally pulls in. We get in, but it's pretty full. By "pretty full" I mean there are barely a few standing places left. The lady tourist asks me if I want to share a taxi again. I redirect the question at Sarah and she doesn't really know, she's drugged up by her Dramamine. We get off the bus and discuss it. We ask some other tourists waiting to get on the bus if they would like to share a taxi and immediately two Asian ladies say yes. The lady is able to negotiate the price down to 6,000 rupees, this now makes it 2,000 rupees per couple, very reasonable.

We get in the taxi and finally at 11:00 am, we are on our way to Ella. The 60-ish km takes around 2 hours of curvy roads. We are descending almost the entire way. The air is getting hotter every minute and it feels amazing. And guess what? It's not raining! Warm and not raining? Simply amazing.

TIP 56 – If you can't get a seat on the bus to and from Nuwara Eliya, the taxi is worth it because the roads are very curvy and it's a tough ride to do standing.

On the way there, we all tell our adventures and where everybody is from, etc. The two Asian ladies are from China and the lady and her boyfriend are Polish, but they currently live in the UK. I always tell people we are from Canada, but I also tell people we currently live in Thailand. When I reveal that we live in Thailand, the Polish lady tells me I have no reasons to complain about the rain! True enough. It still sucks to have all your clothes permanently wet for 2 weeks straight! But for her, this was supposed to be a vacation from the cold, wet United Kingdom. Not quite what they were hoping for.

As we are driving, all of a sudden on the other side of the road appears an army of police vehicles: dozens of police cars and motorcycles, with about 10 SUVs sandwiched in between. This is undoubtedly the President of Sri Lanka coming to Nuwara Eliya for the political campaign. We are all very impressed.

There are a lot of landslides on our way to Ella. We often have to slow down to less than 10 km/h because the road narrows down to one lane for both directions as workers are working to clear the landslides. As we near Ella, the last stretch of road is all dirt and it looks like the last 2 to 3 km was completely destroyed by landslides. It seems that just yesterday the road to Ella was completely closed. Again, we are lucky with our timing.

After about 2 and a half hours, we finally arrive in Ella. The driver drops us off in the middle of town. It's a very small town, so everywhere is walkable. All the tourists say their good byes and good luck for the rest of the trip. During the ride, I consulted my cell phone, so I think I know where our hotel is. However, it seems to be in the middle of nowhere, not very close to any road. Regardless, we start walking in the general direction of the hotel.

TIP 57 – Absolutely consider using the Agoda app. I (Cedric) booked all of our guesthouses through Agoda.com and with their Android application, you see the exact GPS position of each hotel on the map,

which came in absolutely essential during this trip because if you simply look for the hotel on Google maps, it's not precise at all. Addresses and street names are not exactly obvious in Sri Lanka, so the Agoda app has been extremely useful.

The guesthouse is quite a walk from the road, but we finally find it after following several signs, each indicating the hotel is "50 meters" away. As we arrive, we are absolutely blown away by the view. The guesthouse is perched on a cliff, which makes us a bit nervous with all the landslides in the area. (Is the hotel going to fall in the middle of the night? Since you are reading these lines, it did not.) The view is breathtaking.

Sarah goes to bed and I sit on the front porch with my tablet and enjoy the magnificent view in their very comfortable chairs. I take the opportunity to research good restaurants in the city on TripAdvisor. After almost an hour of research, I conclude that there is only 1 good restaurant in the whole town, called Ak Ristoro. It is owned by a Japanese lady, who is the chef. Fusion dishes are served. It has only 5-star reviews on TripAdvisor. It looks really good, I'm excited to tell Sarah.

It's time to eat and so I go wake Sarah. Turns out she slept a little bit. This hotel is pretty good. I'd say second best after Kandy. The bed is good, the room is clean, and the bathroom is big with a nice shower, far away from the toilet.

We head to the restaurant I found. Just before leaving the owner advises us that there is a shortcut to town. As he explains it to us with a series of "go straight, turn right, turn left, go straight, turn left." It sounds quite complicated, but we figure it out. The walk is lovely. We walk through tiny backstreets, a forest loaded with banana and jackfruit trees and a tea plantation until finally we reach the main road to town.

The restaurant looks brand new, very modern and nothing like what we've seen in this country so far. We take a look at the menu and I am impressed. It really is fusion, dishes I have never seen or heard of before. I almost want to try everything on the menu. I go ahead and choose the red bean spaghetti with beef, with a ginger beer. It is absolutely delicious. By very far, the best meal we've had in a restaurant in this country.

TIP 58 – Eat at AK Ristoro for all your non-guesthouse meals in Ella. Otherwise, you are missing out on one of the best restaurants in Sri Lanka.

We are excited to come back here for all our meals in Ella. Especially tomorrow for lunch after climbing Little Adam's Peak as it's not too far on the way back.

This town is very good for our morale: the view is absolutely stunning, we have a comfortable accommodation, and it's not raining! (For the first time in our trip.) The temperature is warmer than in Nuwara Eliya (which feels amazing) and we are able to eat delicious food. We feel very blessed right now. This is what we thought our whole trip would be like. Unfortunately so far, it's been nothing like it, quite the opposite; uncomfortable accommodations, permanent downpour, cold temperature, disgusting food, everything so so sooo expensive, disappointing UNESCO sites. But here, right now, it's good. We're enjoying it. We go to bed satisfied.

DAY 11: SARAH'S TAKE

After a pretty terrible sleep, I wake up to one very sore and dry nasal passage. This is the beginning of a cold. It always starts with one nostril. We go downstairs and have another amazing meal. Loga makes hoppers (like crêpe). She pours liquid batter into a hot pan, goes round to smooth it with the back of ladle, adds some scrambled egg mixture on top with onions and herbs, then flips it to cook the other side, and serve.

It is delicious, I eat 3 or 4, even though I am not that hungry. It's just so good. JP brings coconut sambal and hot roti to the table. Yum, eat some of that. Have another nice chat with German/Chinese couple. This morning, the Chinese woman is openly criticizing the country, how they are all scammers and it is hard to trust anyone. Loga is bustling around the kitchen and seems unaffected by this frank discussion of her countrymen.

JP tells us the tuk tuk should arrive soon. As we leave the table, the Chinese woman corners JP and insists that his home is not in good shape and if he would only renovate the place, it would be much better and he could charge $100/night. JP is not saying much, very unusual for him.

Waiting for the tuk tuk to arrive, I take a double dose of Dramamine pills. I don't want to repeat the foolish mistake of last time. The driver is late and both Loga and JP are calling him on their olde tyme cell and yelling into the phone. After waiting about 40 minutes, Cedric mutters to me, "It only takes 10 minutes to walk to town."

When the tuk tuk finally arrives, he has a jerkoff attitude (as usual). He drives us to the buses. Of course, it's in the same spot as when we arrived: the bus station. There's been no changes to anything.

We ask the tuk tuk which bus and he pretends he doesn't understand, just gestures into the sea of buses parked. Cedric insists, "Which bus to Ella?"

He points to one, I confirm the number on the bus to him, "298?" He says yes, so we pay him and leave. We approach the bus 298, it is empty and no driver.

We are approached by a taxi driver, he says, "Where you go?" My pills are kicking in and I'm drowsy and irritable. Cedric tells him our destination, the guy says we just missed the bus and the next one comes at 11:30, "But how about a tuk tuk, sir?" We can't stop moving or the vampires close in. They say, "Hello," and then ask for money one way or another.

We ask different people and climb into buses asking, "Is this the bus to Ella?" Another taxi driver brings us to the station agent in a small room inside the bus station, we ask him what time and he tells us 10:30 and I ask what bus number, he says 31. I believe it.

TIP 59 – There is usually an employed station agent somewhere in the bus terminal building. He will give you the most accurate bus time and number information. If he feels like it.

We sit and wait in the bus station; it's raining and cold. Many Sri Lankans are wearing a woolen cap and winter jacket. I see another white couple, looking backpacker-y and kind of lost.

I want to ask them if they are going to Ella, I feel that fellow travellers would give us an honest answer. I tend to struggle with conversations on my Dramamine. Stoned and sleepy, I don't say anything. They look over at us from time to time, probably thinking the same thing. We spot a bus park in the stall marked "31." We get up and ask the bus driver, are you going to Ella? No.

Seeing that we're waiting at the same stall, the backpacker lady calls out to us, "Where are you going?" I ask Cedric to talk to her, since I don't trust myself to be coherent. She is also going to Ella. We compare information about where and when the Ella bus should arrive. There is only one bus that goes to Ella. We do the "where are you from?" chat and wait for the bus. I take another Dramamine because it's been almost 90 minutes since I took the first dose and it's already wearing off.

They are Polish, living in the UK. She says they were in Kandy and, even though there is a bus that goes straight to Ella, people at the bus station led them to a bus that ended in Nuwara Eliya (only halfway way to their destination). Being in a state of melodramatic dopiness, my jaw drops at this story. "That's terrible," I blurt out. "You have to transfer and pay twice. And since Kandy is the start of the line, you would have had a good chance of getting a seat in Kandy!" She nods, mostly pleased that I understand their situation, but slightly discouraged to hear it reiterated. I sympathize with them, we know how frustrating it is when you are given the wrong information.

When the packed bus to Ella won't really hold all of us, we decide to split a taxi with some other travellers. I get the passenger seat up front, and since I never get sick if I can look out in the direction that we're travelling, I am overjoyed.

The road has two narrow lanes and is busy. Maybe it's always busy, maybe it's the train cancellations, maybe it's because this time of year is a holiday in Sri Lanka (schools are out until Jan 5). This road snakes down the mountain just like the winding when we arrived by bus. The difference is that this driver is great and it's a smooth ride. He doesn't brake and accelerate like a mad man. So I can keep my eyes open and observe what I missed on the ride up; beautiful green mountains and terraced fields.

They are having a great chat in the back. It's always fun meeting with unpretentious young travellers. In the front, I miss out on all the laughing and conversing. I certainly can't risk turning around. I'm too dopey from my pills to contribute coherently, so I listen to the driver as he shows me some highlights. He points out the landslides that spill out onto the road. I am impressed at how well and quickly they have cleared the roads. We see graters everywhere, which also surprised me. I didn't expect them to be so organized and equipped.

It seems like we should be in the middle of nowhere, there are just farms and the occasional house. But small sheet metal shacks are selling a variety of goods on the side of the road. We see quite a few people walking and biking along the roads, so they must live around here. Large rocks are arranged on the asphalt to indicate that the land underneath the road has fallen away. All that's visible is slight cracking in the asphalt, so good thing they put the rocks. I see people standing on the balcony of a house resting on an unstable edge that is falling away.

We arrive at our destination and separate from our new friends. Cedric and I walk on foot to our destination. As Cedric checks his phone, people ask if we need any help. We refuse them all because we are on guard. In our experience so far, everyone who initiates conversation wants money. As we keep walking, we discover people are friendlier here. They say hello and go about their business without asking for anything. Along the road, we pass by a hotel and a woman says hello in excellent English. I look up and it's the Chinese lady from JP's house! She is standing on the balcony of a hotel and waving at us. Small world.

The final 50 feet to the Green Hill Guesthouse is a narrow dirt path along the side of a mountain. This path is not just a little crazy. Luggage with wheels? Vertigo? Walking back to the hotel drunk? Forget about it. They'd find you down at the bottom of the cliff. We approach the side of the hotel, as the front of the hotel faces the valley below. Behind the hotel, they are clearing away fallen soil. A small part of me worries about sliding down the cliff in my sleep.

The hotel is lovely, clean and recently renovated. It's has two floors and we are on the top level. The rooms are back along the mountain and in front is a large covered terrace, completely open for absolutely one of the most beautiful views I've ever seen. Stunning, panoramic. Pictures won't do it justice.

We are not far from the mountain across the valley and at a lower elevation. I observe the activity in the valley below; rushing waterfall, honking vehicles on the main highway heading south and terraced farming.

The view opens up to the south. They say that on a clear day you can see all the way to the ocean. It's very cloudy, but we do see the mountains extend quite far and eventually flatten in the south.

We sit as they prepare our room and feel warm for the first time in over a week. I can't believe this view. Someone is spreading out freshly washed laundry onto the lower balcony roof. It doesn't budge because there is hardly any wind up in these mountains.

I am so groggy from my triple dose of motion sickness pills, lack of sleep and beginnings of a cold, that I can't keep my eyes open. It's a shame to have to leave this beautiful view, but when our room is finally ready, I head to bed.

Cedric lets me rest two hours and I feel less drugged. We head to TripAdvisor's #1 restaurant at around 4 pm because we didn't have lunch (I was sleeping). Taking the back way, we pass a small house with a bunch of puppies out on the road. The restaurant is in a removed location where you pass cows, laundry drying on rocks and people bathing in a stream, on the street to the restaurant.

We head inside and it is a beautiful, elegant décor. Everything on the menu looks wonderful and they have our favourite EGB (Elephant House Ginger Beer). The food turns out to be excellent and a great price, especially considering the quality. Cedric has a kind of spaghetti bolognese with ground beef, red kidney beans and a hint of cinnamon/cloves in the tomato sauce. I have a Japanese style, soy sauce steamed chicken spaghetti topped with seaweed. We are both very happy with the place and decide to eat there for lunch and dinner tomorrow.

DAY 12: DECEMBER 29, 2014

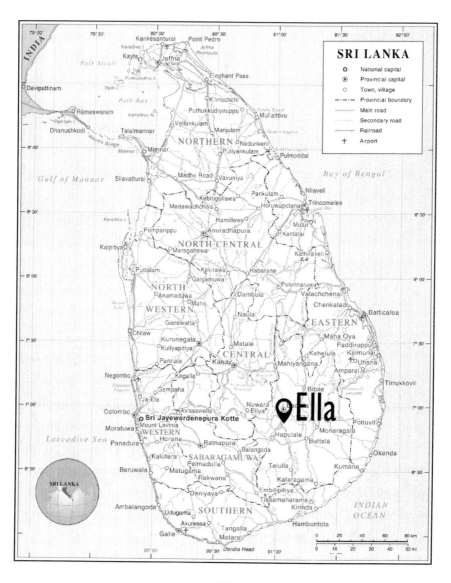

Today we're excited to hike Little Adam's Peak. We get up at around 9 am and go sit on the porch, waiting for breakfast to be served. Breakfast is ok but not great, as usual. Right after breakfast we leave for Little Adam's Peak. It's only a 15-minute walk to the base of the mountain and then another 20-25 minutes to the peak. The walk to the Peak is lovely. You go through a pretty big tea plantation and witness Tamils picking tea leaves. It's really awesome.

Unfortunately, just as we reached the top, it got really cloudy. There was essentially no view and we were literally in the clouds. But that didn't matter because it was the walk there that was awesome and we already had a breathtaking view from our hotel porch so it didn't matter at all.

Going down, I am looking forward to a bite at our new favorite restaurant Ak Ristoro. On the way down (or up, it's the same path) you can take a small detour to go have a drink or a meal at another restaurant set in the mountains. You can also go visit a green tea plantation nearby. There are signs to guide you. We decided to not go as it was already time for lunch and we really wanted to go back to Ak Ristoro. However, once at Ak Ristoro, we are greeted with an unpleasant surprise. The restaurant has a piece of paper taped to the door that reads "Sorry Today is closed".

Let me tell you how disappointed I am. Actually there are no words to describe how disappointed I am. I am ridiculously disappointed. What a downer. The best restaurant by far that we've eaten at in the country, that I was so looking forward to eat at twice today, is closed...

We walk to town and don't really know what to do. When the taxi dropped us off on our way into town, we saw quite a few nice-looking restaurants with a patio on the main road, so we decide to simply go to one of those. We are hungry but none of the restaurants have good reviews on TripAdvisor. If we had known we probably would have eaten at one of the restaurants on the way back down from the mountain.

We reach a restaurant that looks alright. We order a margarita pizza. It is absolutely disgusting. The rest of the day is uneventful, we rest at the hotel in the afternoon. In the evening, we eat at that same crap restaurant downtown. Even though we avoid meat and order the veggie burger, Sarah gets sick from it and I don't feel so good. It's the first time on this trip that we've been sick from the food. We are not looking forward to tomorrow as we are anticipating a long bus ride to Tissamaharama. As happy as we were yesterday, today we feel low. But the view is helping smooth things out.

TIP 60 – Make sure your Ella guesthouse has an outstanding view. It's an experience beyond compare and not much difference in price.

DAY 12: SARAH'S TAKE

Breakfast this morning is a pot of coffee (for me) and tea (for Cedric), egg hoppers (bowl shaped crêpe with fried egg cooked inside), coconut sambal, dal, string hoppers, and fresh fruit. Savoury, spicy and a typical Sri Lankan breakfast, I like it. Cedric is not impressed. We sit and enjoy an amazing view of the valley.

After we eat, the guesthouse owner asks about our next destination, Tissamaharama (which they often call Tissa). We ask about taking the bus and he explains that there are a couple of transfers involved. He says he can get us a taxi for 6000 rupees and that there is lots to see on the way. He brings out a binder filled with computer printouts of attractions in plastic cover sheets. He opens it to a waterfall and talks about some other things to see on the drive to Tissa. We are wary, since these "on the way" attractions usually cost a lot and the driver gets a commission. We ask him if he knows any other travellers heading to Tissa tomorrow, he says he will make some inquiries.

He tells us that we should hurry to Little Adam's Peak for our hike because it's only clear early and starts to get cloud cover in the late morning.

Little Adam's Peak is a fairly high peak on our side of the valley and gives an amazing panoramic view of the area. My one sore nostril spread to my sinuses and I have a small fever and lots of sniffles, so I bring lots of Kleenex with me.

TIP 61 – In Ella, head to Little Adam's Peak early morning before the clouds roll in. Let your host know the night before what your plans are and see if they can have breakfast ready early.

There isn't too much signage, but we trust Google maps and walk along a main road for 10-15 minutes. We finally arrive at a sign and see old woman and little girl in front of us and two police officers walking a path up a hill. As we are about to pass the old woman, she turns around and puts out her hand, "Have money." The 5-year-old girl mimics the pose and phrase.

We say, "Sorry, no," and keep walking. She keeps repeating the phrase as we pass her until we are well in front of her.

The path up to the Peak is through a tea plantation. We see Tamil women picking tea leaves. They have a towel folded on their head which supports a cord attached to an open bag resting on their back. As they rapidly pick from the little thorny bushes, they reach back and drop the leaves into the open sack.

As we near the centre of plantation there are a few metal shacks bunched together and Indian dance music is blasting from somewhere. It's a fun atmosphere. The Tamil women chat with each other as they work. They smile at us as we walk by and say hello. They don't ask for money, they are just very friendly and go about their business. Stepping into the middle of a tea plantation is such an unexpected surprise. The tea shrubs are growing up steep hills with sharp angles. The women work quickly and move like ghosts among the bushes. The hike is a nice low intensity, but my fever has me feeling tired and weak. We approach the last leg of the hike and it's quite a steep climb up crumbling stairs, some of which are washed out near the top.

TIP 62 – Definitely visit Little Adam's Peak. If you can't do steep climbs, just walk until the base of the Peak. The tea planation that you walk through is just as interesting, if not more, than the Peak itself.

I'm exhausted when we reach the Peak and my sinuses are giving me a headache. I constantly have a Kleenex in my face, blowing my nose. By the time we reach the summit, the clouds have rolled in and we are surrounded by mist. Cedric points out that we see more from our hotel (because it isn't in the clouds). When a gust of wind blows, we see the backside of the mountain our hotel is on. There is a green tea factory and restaurant nearby. At the very top of the rock are two stray dogs and some Hindu/Buddhist flags. One of them hobbles around with a broken hind leg. The dogs look pretty skinny and I wonder what they eat.

I get dizzy walking back down the steps. We cross an intersecting path and a sign indicating the green tea factory offers tours. Cedric asks me if I want to go. It would be interesting, but I am so hot, sweaty, thirsty, and tired, that I don't really care. I tell Cedric that if he wants to go, I'll go too. But we decide we'll just head down the hill and go to our new favourite restaurant for lunch.

TIP 63 – Bring some water or buy a bottle from one of the little kiosks on your Little Adam's Peak walk. Climbing the Peak itself is a workout.

We are both looking forward to trying something new on the menu because it had tons of interesting things without a singular theme, like a brainstorm of every favourite food. Upon arrival, we discover that they are closed all day. Cedric is devastated, so much so that I can hardly believe he is being serious. We head into town to eat.

Sitting on a patio overlooking the main road, we order ginger beer and pizza. They bring us Lion brand ginger beer, which tastes like Sprite with pepper (i.e. awful). Cedric reads "nature identical ginger beer flavor" on ingredients list and we have a lively discussion about food labeling regulations. We look up and see the Polish couple from our taxi ride walking up the street; they wave to us. I wonder where they are staying and if it is as nice as our hotel. The pizza is terrible. Like a large, thin cracker with bland sauce and non-existent cheese.

We head back to the hotel still hungry and disappointed. We pass a man offering taxi service, he says 6,500 rupees to Tissa. We ask if he has any other clients to split the cab with and he says no, but he takes our number just in case. Even one other couple would significantly reduce the cost.

I have a sinus headache, so I rest back at the hotel. We hope to eat at the guesthouse for supper, but they start serving food around 8 pm. Since we are still hungry from lunch, we head out at 5-ish. We check the reviews of every passing restaurant and none are good. We try a café on the main road. Its patio is covered, but lower than street level. We walk down the stairs and sit down, the server brings us menus. Chairs are wrought iron and uncomfortable. Menu is more expensive than at lunch and it smells like exhaust and garbage, as the street smells descend to basement level. I hate it, so we walk out and head to the café next door, the same Chill Café of today's lunch.

From our table, I can see the cook staff. One guy is tossing fries in a stainless steel bowl with his hands and putting them on a plate. Another guy is standing around picking at his face with his fingers. I wonder what I can order that will have minimal bacterial content. Something well cooked, without too much handling.

I suggest the steak with sautéed veg, thinking it will be safer. It's 850 rupees and we can split it. Cedric isn't interested, so we order veggie burgers. There is a little corgi dog walking around the restaurant pleading for scraps with silent eyes. It's a fat little dog, so the begging must work. The veggie burger is fried dal patty and it tastes old. I am sure this is leftovers from the expensive 10-course Sri Lankan curry meals offered on their menu.

Back at the hotel, we ask the owner if he found any other guests to split the taxi to Tissa. He says everyone cancelled and we are the only people in the hotel right now. After an hour, I start to feel ill. I throw up several times (damn that veggie burger!) and go to bed feeling pretty low.

DAY 13: DECEMBER 30, 2014

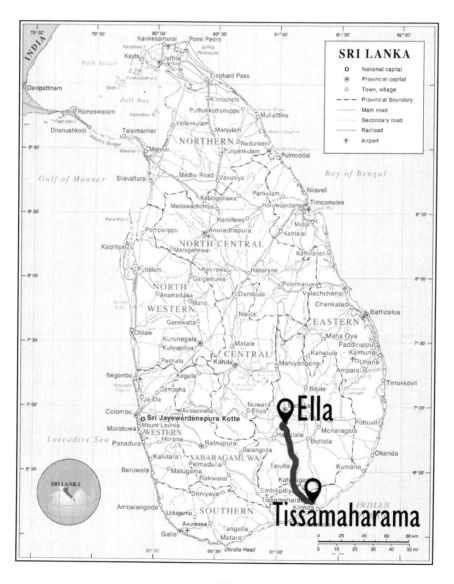

Today is my birthday. It sucks. I'm probably going to have the worst birthday in my life. We're planning on taking a long bus ride, probably standing the whole way for around 3 hours. Taking a taxi would cost $60. We're on a budget and can't afford to take a taxi between each destination. We're also not looking forward to our next hotel as our current one is one of the best; it can only get worse, not better. I make sure to have a shower this morning. You never know if your next hotel is going to have hot water. It hasn't happened on our trip so far, but experience tells me to always expect the worst in this country. I am usually a very optimistic person, but it seems like the worst happens most of the time here. When good things occasionally happen, it's a delightful surprise.

Everybody cancelled their reservation because of the landslides and the cancelled trains, so no luck trying to find other travellers at our hotel! We eat breakfast, which is disgusting, and we head out, hoping to find other travellers around the bus stop.

Unfortunately, there is nobody at the bus stop either. The town isn't dead; there are quite a few tourists everywhere, just not at the bus stop and not at our hotel. Sarah asks a few random tourists on the street if they are arriving or leaving, they are all arriving. I think because the road just reopened a couple of days ago, more tourists are coming in, but nobody is leaving yet. I don't know... Just trying to invent some theory as to why we can't seem to find anybody else taking the bus this morning, there are so many tourists in this town.

TIP 64 – If you want to take a taxi, be sure to ask other travellers at the hotel and at the bus stop if they are going to the same place and split the fare.

As we are waiting at the bus stop, a man approaches us and asks where we are going. We tell him Tissa, but we highly suspect he is a taxi driver and we can't afford his services. Next thing you know, he asks if we need a taxi. We both tell him we can't afford it. He asks, "How much can you afford?"

We both say "$30."

He says, "Ok $40." We pause for a second. I say $30 again. He says, "No. The other drivers in town sell it for $60. I give it to you for $40." I think again for a moment and we decide to take his offer. It's a victory. A small one, but a victory nonetheless. You get very few victories in this country. Before confirming, we ask to actually see his taxi. We want to make sure it's not a tuk tuk or a small vehicle. It's a minivan, looks pretty good. We get in.

On the ride there, we find out the taxi driver is from Tissa. So he was most likely heading back to Tissa anyway, with customers or not, hence the deal. The taxi driver asks us if it's ok to stop 2 minutes so he can buy vegetables. Sure, why not. He gets back in the van without buying anything. Says it's too expensive because the landslides damaged the crops. Interesting piece of local life. On the way there, we pass a few buses, all completely full. I am thankful for this ride because the alternative is standing in a hot crowded bus for 3 hours. The best $40 I've spent in a long time. Speaking of hot, it is. It's getting hotter by the minute as we descend the mountains. We went from 1 km above sea level to sea level. It's hot, really hot. We haven't been hot on this trip, except on the first day in Colombo. It's sunny too, it's beautiful.

After a couple of hours, we reach our hotel. We are welcomed with glasses of fresh watermelon juice. Delicious. On the house too, so it tastes even more delicious. Unfortunately, our room is not ready, but we are hungry and this hotel has a nice big open patio restaurant. We sit and order some food. I get the stir fried chicken noodle. Delicious. And guess what? It's cheap. Only $2 for a plate of food. Unbelievable. Delicious food for cheap. Are we still in Sri Lanka I wonder?

After our food we inquire about the safari. I'm really unsure whether I want to do it or not. It would be silly not to go because this whole detour to Tissa was just for the safari. There is nothing else to see or do. Everybody comes here for the safari. I'm hesitant because I'm afraid it's going to be another one of those expensive nothing-to-see attraction. For two people, the whole safari is around $120. Quite expensive. We decide to do it and hope for the best.

The safari itself is around 5 to 6 hours on a jeep with a guide. We go through Yala National Park and drive around and hope to see crocodiles, elephants, monkeys, leopards among others. The star of the show is the leopard, but we are advised chances of seeing one are slim. We hop on the jeep and go. The National Park is actually 30 minutes from our hotel. As we drive through, I notice this town is very different from any other we've visited in this country so far. It looks richer. There are a lot of motorbikes on the road. The food is also cheap so this makes me feel more like we are in Thailand. However, once we arrive in the National Park that's when the fun stops.

The roads in the park are atrocious. They are so bumpy it's unbelievable. For 6 hours straight we are bouncing almost like if you are on a vibrating bed but 10 times more intense. I am hating every minute of it. For me, this is worse than taking an airplane and I hate taking the plane.

At least we got to see some animals. We saw some birds. We saw a crocodile. We saw an elephant and monkeys. All things I can already see on a daily basis in Thailand on my way to school. Alright, I don't see any crocodiles and elephants on my way to school, but I do see monkeys and birds.

Anyway, we basically didn't get to see much. Just a very bouncy ride that's giving me a huge headache after 5 hours of bouncing. Definitely the worst birthday.

We get back to the hotel at around 6 pm and go eat at the hotel's restaurant. We order some more traditional Sri Lankan food and it is very good. But the food takes an eternity to arrive and we end up eating at around 8 pm. Most people eat at that time anyways so it's no big deal. We go to bed right after dinner.

TIP 65 – Though we suspect that these Sri Lankan curry meals are just reheated dishes, they often take 60 to 90 minutes to reach your table. Something to consider before ordering it from the menu.

The room we have is very basic, but we only paid $20, so at least we are satisfied with the value. The bathroom is very basic with no hot water. I'll have a shower tomorrow at the next hotel. Speaking of which, our next hotel is supposed to be one of the best hotel we've reserved in this country as it is one of the most expensive. Even with this fact, I've learned to never expect anything good in this country.

Today was the worse birthday of my life, but I don't have time to feel bad about it. I don't really care all that much about my birthday anyways. But it would have been nice to have an ok day. Right now, all I can think of is the extremely long bus ride to Galle (pronounced "goal" for some reason). Galle is quite far. The longest distance we've had to do by bus. The only good news is it's going to be the last one. The biggest, but the last. The last big nail on the coffin, it's a very big one. It's supposed to take around 5 hours by bus. I'm tired now. Going to bed.

DAY 13: SARAH'S TAKE

I have a terrible sleep. I toss and turn, feeling like I'm going to throw up again. I wake up feeling unwell, unrested and unhappy. We need to leave today and I am depressed at the bus ride ahead of us. We head out to the balcony for a beautiful view and breakfast.

Breakfast is a disaster. It's an eggy crêpe wrapped around caramelized banana. It should be delicious, but it tastes and smells like soggy old dish towels. So we don't eat much. There is a gigantic black pup at the hotel, the only guest we've seen, and he joins us for breakfast.

Cedric says it would be a good time to Skype back home. I feel sick and don't want to talk to anyone. I just want to sit in peace and enjoy the view. Cedric calls his mom on Skype and she wishes him a happy birthday. Oops! I completely forgot it was his birthday today. And I've been such a grouch this morning.

I take a whole bunch of Dramamine for our upcoming trip and pretty much black out for the rest of the day until we reach our new hotel.

On the taxi ride to Tissa, we pass a huge waterfall. There are monkeys all over the road, lots of vendors and people. Our driver slows down near the waterfall and asks if he wants us to stop. It is lovely and we probably should have stopped because there are so many tourists and it would be a free activity, but I say no. I just want to get to our destination because I'm so tired. The problem about being drugged all the time is that I'm always tired. I am also a little nauseous on this ride and press on my pressure points.

TIP 66 – The advantage of hiring a taxi driver between destinations is that you can make stops along the way or go buy some supplies at a store. Don't forget to take advantage of that.

When we exit the mountains, it is much warmer and a straighter, smoother ride. So I feel a little better. As we pass through the towns and countryside of the south, things seem a little duller and less green. Coconut trees have yellow tinged leaves and some trees are completely bare, seemingly dead. The dirt isn't the vibrant red ochre of the north, but dusty beige.

We arrive at the Lake Edge Holiday Inn in Tissa and I'm impressed. Like the name suggests, it is at the edge of a lake. Actually, it's on a strip of parkland sandwiched between two lakes. The yard is lovely with hammocks and seating areas. It's the nicest yard yet. Although, maybe all the guesthouse yards have been this nice, but with the pouring rain I wasn't able to see it very well. A server comes out of kitchen and we are greeted with a glass of watermelon smoothie (pureed watermelon and some water to loosen it). Delicious. A woman helps us get signed in and I am feeling happy to have such a wonderful welcome and friendliness.

In a moment of uncharacteristic gregariousness, I exclaim that it's Cedric's birthday today. She asks how old and I ask how old does she think. She says 24. We laugh and I say 30, she is shocked. She explain the different safaris available. This afternoon 2:00 - 6:30 pm, costs 4500 for jeep + 2800 per ticket. Tomorrow morning 4:30 am – 9:00 am, it's more expensive for jeep, 5500 rupees. However, the jeep seats 6 people, so the cost of the jeep can be split. This afternoon there is no one else, so we'd take on the whole cost. Its Cedric's birthday, so I tell him to pick whatever he wants. She tells us no one saw the leopard on this morning's run, but it's a nice afternoon we might have a better chance of seeing something. We pick 2 pm and ask if they serve lunch. She says as long as we pick something quick like fried rice or noodles. Our room is not quite ready yet (fudge I have to pee).

TIP 67 – It seems like no matter what time you arrive, the room is never ready. Expect to wait around 30 to 60 minutes before you can access the room. If you have somewhere to go, you can usually leave your bags with the host.

We order chicken fried noodles and ask if they have EGB. She says yes, but brings Lion brand (Coca Cola) back to the table. We tell her it was supposed to be EGB and she says it's the same. We say it's not and she is shocked that we can taste a difference. It takes a good 25 minutes for our food to arrive at the table. The safari jeep has arrived before our food. They forgot to add the chicken, but the food is tasty, not overly salted and bland like we've been having.

After eating, we head to the room to quickly get changed and pee. The lady tells us if we hurry we can spend more time in the park and it is better for us. We are not sure this makes sense, but we get ready as quickly as we can and head out to the jeep.

Our driver is gone, I look into the jeep's front seat and see there is someone in the passenger seat, I smile and say hello. He just looks at me and doesn't say anything. I say we are ready to go. He still just looks at me unsmiling. I think…ok another happy employee. I turn around and see the driver coming out of the kitchen with some water bottles. He sees us and approaches smiling. He helps us into the back of the jeep, which is elevated. It's so fun to have the whole ride to ourselves. We have a great view from all sides, no legroom though.

We are not two minutes from the hotel when the driver stops and points. He says something we can't understand and get him to repeat it several times, until I look where he's pointing and see thousands of giant bats hanging from a cluster of trees. The trees are huge and the bats are fairly large lumps hanging off the branches. Then he points out a crocodile sitting on a rock and soaking up the sun. This is just next to our hotel!

As we drive through the city toward the National Park, I see lots of jeeps headed in the same direction. Many of them empty, with only a couple of people, just like ours. The drive to the park is longer than I expected. We finally enter the park, through a little gate, attended by a security guard. We pass a house and on the front lawn (I should say "front dirt" as there is no lawn in sight) is a big, beautiful peacock is strutting across. The peacock's head is gleaming iridescent-blue with long, lovely tail feathers. I am so captivated by its beauty that I don't think to take a photo.

TIP 68 – Always take photos, even when you're hesitant (religious sites). Perhaps momentarily unpleasant, later you will be glad you have the picture.

We approach an area full of parked jeeps and an office, this must be the payment area. Cedric exits the jeep with the driver and 6000 rupees (I guess there's tax on the 2800 rupee ticket). I move back one seat, wanting to see if there is more legroom elsewhere in the jeep. Looking around, there are people in parked jeeps, people in line for washroom, lots of little buildings. I glance back to the jeep cabin and the second guy is staring at me. When I make eye contact, he smiles and says hello. (Well, he's finally put on his customer service hat.) I say hello back and he keeps quiet, but stares at me until Cedric and the driver return. (I liked him better when he was grumpy.) I'm glad I moved back one seat.

The driver does a good job of pointing things out to us and naming them, so we know what we are seeing. We are seeing some wild animals up close and I am having an awesome time. I am trying to take pictures, but the roads are flooded and bumpy, so most of my shots are blurry. When an elephant is spotted, there is a mad rush of jeeps to the best lookout spot. I am happy that this is a birthday that Cedric will always remember.

The sun starts to set and we head back to the hotel. We order our Sri Lankan curry dinner. It takes forever to reach our table. Turns out Cedric absolutely hated the safari and thinks it was a huge waste of money. Darn.

TIP 69 – If you go on the Yala National Park safari, consider wearing dark clothes and shower thoroughly afterward. Open jeep plus red dirt roads equals filthy.

DAY 14: DECEMBER 31, 2014

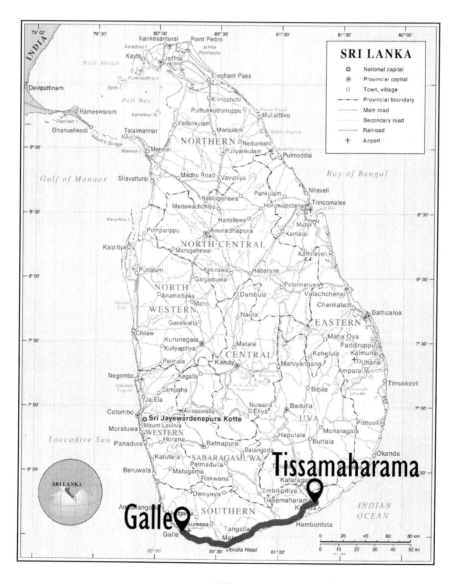

Today we're already leaving for our next and final destination: Galle. We took our Ella-Tissa taxi driver's phone number in case we wanted to take a taxi to Galle. He offered $70 and he says that's a deal, normally it's $80. I almost want to do it but Sarah doesn't. I know she's right. We just spent a fortune on the safari and shouldn't be taking taxis between each destination because it really adds up. This time we have to suffer.

We have breakfast and take a tuk tuk to the bus station. We have to take a bus to Matara and then another one to Galle. Thankfully, the bus for Matara is almost empty and we get to sit. Phew, we won't be standing up for the next 4 or 5 hours. But even sitting becomes uncomfortable after several hours. There is not much leg room at all, similar to a school bus. During the trip I have an epiphany. I finally realise why these buses don't have any leg room. The only head sticking out of the seat in the whole bus is mine. These Sri Lankans are very—and I mean very—short. There are not very many men taller than 5'5" and the women are mostly around 5'. I am 6-12 inches taller than everyone. There is no leg room on the bus, not because they are too poor to afford it, but because they don't need it. I'm only 5'11" and I feel like a giant in this country.

The trip is very long. The bus stops all of the time. We rarely go more than 10 minutes without the bus stopping to pick up or drop off passengers. But after 4 hours, we finally arrive in Matara. There are no bathroom on these buses. I purposely don't drink much water so I don't have to go. But right now, I am very thirsty, the south is much warmer than anywhere we've been so far in this country.

We are at the Matara bus station. It's very big. For the first time in this country, I see a lot of modern coach buses and I feel like I travelled in the future. They are not predominant, most of the buses are the usual Sri Lankan ones, but I can see 3 or 4 of them. I look to see if any of them are going to Galle, but they are not. It's not that far, only 1 more hour, so we just go ahead and try to find the regular bus for Galle. The bus is almost empty, only 1 other person on board and the driver is not there so we can't ask the driver to confirm. We sit and hope.

After 10 minutes the bus is filling up a bit more and the driver comes and board and we depart. As we are driving to Galle, we are realizing that this bus is basically a city bus. It is stopping every 1-2 minutes. We wonder if maybe there was a more express bus to Galle. There probably was if we had looked more. The trip takes around 2 hours…At least we have a seat. At some point in time the bus fills up so much that even seated I am being squished.

I noticed there are a lot of signs in the south that say "No Honking." Seems like I'm not the only one who finds it utterly annoying.

We arrive at Galle bus station mid-afternoon. It's been a long trip. We are thirsty, hungry and tired. Thankfully, the bus stop is only a 5-minute walk to the Fort and 10-12 minute walk to our hotel, which is inside the Fort. We prefer to walk as opposed to taking a tuk tuk as we are tired of getting screwed, and it's only another 15 minutes.

We arrive at our hotel, which was really easy to find, thanks to the awesome Agoda app. We are showed our room, which is on the first floor, right beside the lobby and the common area. There are huge French doors that give onto the common area with a curtain that doesn't cover the whole window/door. The first impression of this room is bad. The room is tiny with no privacy. However, the bathroom is nice and big.

We're hungry, so we immediately go out. I previously researched restaurants in Galle and thankfully there are at least 3-4 good restaurants in the fort. They are outrageously expensive, but I don't care at this point, I just want to eat good food. It's been really hard to eat good food in this country. We decide to go to Rocket Burger, a burger joint. Haven't had a burger in a while, so why not? The burgers turn out to be absolutely delicious. Expensive, but delicious, feels very good to eat such delicious food.

After lunch, we just walk around and visit the fort. In the Fort, you really feel like you are not in Sri Lanka anymore. The main religion in the Fort is Muslim, so you have the mosque yelling out at different moments during the day. There are a lot of Muslims in the Fort. This is a very big contrast from the rest of the country, where you don't see many Muslims at all. The streets are clean and nice-looking, narrow but clean. Again, a very big contrast from outside the fort.

There are so many tourists of all ethnicities in the fort: Asians, Europeans, Australians, Indians, etc. The fort reminds me a lot of Quebec City, which feels nice and familiar. I feel like I am back in civilization. We are in Galle for 3 nights. I thought we could use the break after a long backpacking trip across the country. I thought right. It's nice to just relax and stay at the same place for a while. The only problem is our hotel is total crap. And I really mean it.

We go back to our hotel later in the afternoon and I decide to go have a shower. There is a big window in the shower (as with almost all the guest houses we stayed at), but the only difference here is that normally on the other side of the window you don't have much, it's just the back of the building where nobody really hangs out. But in this case, on the other side of the window you have an outdoor bathroom that the owners are using. As I was going to have a shower, I see someone having a shower on the other side of the window. There is just this big window that allows you and them to see in each other's bathroom! So not only don't you have any privacy in the bedroom, but you don't have any in the bathroom either!

Today is December 31, but we are so tired from our day and from our trip in general that we don't even know if we're going to make it to midnight. We only had a small $7 burger for lunch and are still both hungry. It's around supper time and we head out to another recommended restaurant on TripAdvisor, called Crêpe-ology. It has rave reviews on TripAdvisor. Sarah says she's not hungry, but probably just wants to save money. She orders a side of hummus. I order the Huevos Rancheros and an Italian soda. It was absolutely amazing, the eggs were cooked and seasoned to perfection, simply amazing, I am highly impressed. It's quite expensive, but I don't mind paying when it's that delicious. We go back to our hotel highly satisfied, but a bit depressed by how uncomfortable our hotel room is.

It's hot, so we try to turn on the air conditioning. Nothing happens; it doesn't work. It's already late, we'll notify the owners tomorrow. Midnight is approaching and we are in our bed watching movies on our tablet. Lame, but we are tired. There is so much noise around that we can't go to sleep. It's New Year's Eve, can't really complain about the noise, we are the lame ones staying in our hotel room on New Year's Eve. Midnight rings and we can hear fireworks going off. They don't sound like huge fireworks, but they sound pretty big, probably medium-sized ones. So tired that I don't even bother going outside to attempt taking a look at them. An hour later or so, the noise is reduced and I finally fall asleep.

DAY 14: SARAH'S TAKE

The hotel has several breakfast options at their restaurant, but we just order the cheapest item: omelette. It arrives and it's HUGE, so we only finish half. I guess we could have split one. The hotel staff arranges a tuk tuk to the bus station. She explains what bus to take to Galle and that because of the holiday, it might be busy. The tuk tuk arrives 20 minutes later to take us to the bus station.

TIP 70 – Many tuk tuk drivers are slow to pick you up from the guesthouse when called. Plan for that tardiness.

The music blasting on the bus is more soothing, probably because the driver and attendant are much older gentlemen. I am doped up and have my eyes closed for the bus ride, but Cedric makes me open them to check out the beach. We are travelling along the southern coast and the long stretches of sandy beaches are lovely. When we arrive in Matara at the bus station, it's very busy. There are buses all over the place, more than we've ever seen here. We walk up and down the bus station, almost getting run over. They all seem to say Galle...so we ask the driver who is standing outside his bus which one we should take and he gestures up at the front. I guess the buses are all going to the same places, just the ones at the front leave first.

We arrive in Galle, hot as hell, and walk into the walled fort on foot. There's a huge sound system set up near the cricket field playing some Sri Lankan/Indian hip hop. It has English lyrics and I try to memorize what they are saying to Google the song later, but after an hour of researching I don't find the song and the lyrics escape me.

Walking through Galle to our hotel, I find it very charming. The brick roads in the fort are narrow, giving everything a compact feel. The buildings are generally two storeys, so the fort has an open feel. It's an interesting mix. There are entirely renovated high-end hotels, restaurants and shops. There are convenience stores in decaying buildings. There are derelict concrete constructions, oddly abandoned in such a touristy area.

Among all of these are local residences, usually fairly run down, with laundry drying on the front balcony. I see a lot of older people in these residences, many of them Muslims. ("I see" because most of them have their door open and are sitting on a chair, looking out onto the street.) The only annoying thing about Galle is that we constantly have to move out of the way for a honking tuk tuk or car. This place would be 100 times better if they would make it a pedestrian area, only allowing vehicles for delivery. It's such a small area that you can walk everywhere in 10 minutes.

We check-in at the Secret Palace Guesthouse and our room is dreadful. They close-off a section of the living room and voilà, our bedroom. Our tiniest room yet, we can barely fit our bags and walk to the bathroom (the bathroom is disproportionately very large). Windowed French doors are covered with a gaping curtain…this is our wall from the living room. Obviously, everyone can see directly into our room and bed from the comfort of their couch. I try to adjust things so that we have more privacy. The TV in the living room is hanging on the wall of our room, so the speakers blare directly into our room. Above the door to our room is decorated glass, which lines up with a flight of stairs, so that people can see into our room as they descend the stairs. Our bathroom window has a bar placed so the window can't be shut, so it lets in tons of mosquitoes. Speaking of mosquitoes, the room is FULL of them and the mosquito net doesn't really close perfectly.

We go eat a sloppy BBQ chicken sandwich and veggie burger. The meal is tasty, but a little pricy at $7-8 per small burger. I am exhausted and don't remember the rest of the day. I remember eating some tasty hummus at Crêpe-ology. It's New Year's Eve and they have fireworks, but we hop in bed, exhausted. The hotel is empty because everyone is out partying. Even the family is out and there is finally no TV sound. It's nice. Then at around 1 am people filter in and loudly wish "Happy New Year." Someone arrives at 3 am and rings the buzzer over and over again until the staff unlocks the front door. Like the TV, this buzzer must also be attached to our wall because it is insanely loud.

DAY 15: JANUARY 1, 2015

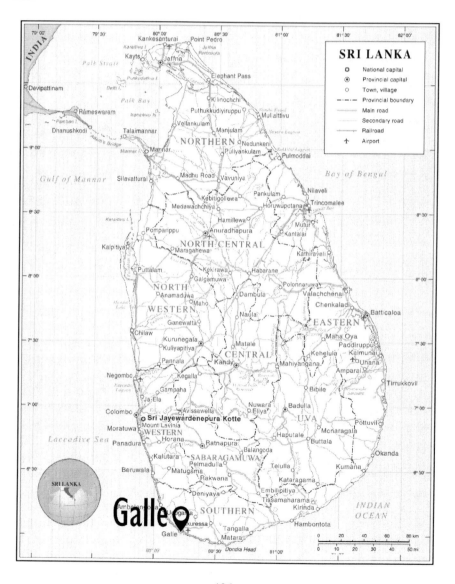

It's around 3 am and I am being woken up by a super loud buzzer. Is there a fire? My heart is pounding. The buzzer stops and goes. It sounds like it's the doorbell. It appears like they lock the door at night, so every time someone arrives in the middle of the night they have to ring the buzzer to wake up the owner (and us in the process). This hotel is really starting to piss me off. I know it's New Year's Eve, but this hotel just sucks. There is zero privacy in the bedroom and in the bathroom, you get woken up by buzzers in the middle of the night, the air conditioning doesn't work. I wonder what will be next...

This morning we wake up relatively early for New Year's Day. It gets quite bright early as there is a huge window in our room with no curtain. It's also very noisy as the common area is just on the other side of our French doors in our room. Those have a curtain, but it doesn't cover up the whole door/window. I can't believe I booked this hotel for 3 nights! This is the most nights I booked in the whole country and it has to be at such an uncomfortable place.

TIP 71 – Galle is interesting but small, so don't plan for more than 2 days in the fort or else you may get bored.

We leave our room for breakfast. The owner tells us to go upstairs and asks if we want tea or coffee. Breakfast arrives and it is atrocious. Definitely the worst breakfast we had in the whole country. My omelette is burnt, the fruits are so unripe they are hard as a rock. We barely eat anything. We decide to go walk the entire perimeter of the Fort, it's supposed to be a scenic walk. We are walking on the wall that surrounds the Fort, the view is indeed beautiful, mostly endless kilometres of ocean.

As we get to the north portion of the wall, we get a good view of the Cricket Stadium just north of the Fort. I look on my smart phone to get more information about the Cricket Stadium. I read it is of international standards and has a capacity of 35,000 people. This is quite a surprising fact because looking at the stadium, I really don't see very many seats, maybe 5000. Maybe people sit in the grass at the extremity of the stadium and they count these people in the capacity. But as with most things we've experienced in this country so far, it wouldn't surprise me if this was a complete lie.

The walls of the Fort are in a state of disrepair, it doesn't seem like the government is maintaining it very much at all. Sometimes we reach nicer portions of the wall with a sign indicating that this portion of the wall is graciously maintain by X company. Since entry to the Fort is free, it doesn't surprise me. But actually, even if there was a fee to enter the Fort, the walls would most likely still be in this same disrepair, as were most of the other paying sites we visited in this country.

We head to Crêpe-ology to cool off and eat an early lunch. With a cheesy quesadilla and large chunks of meaty chicken, Crêpe-ology turns out to be a pure delight once again. We actually hang out there a while. They have couches, free Wi-Fi and amazing food. It's a good opportunity to work on our laptops and just relax.

For supper we decide to try another restaurant that is well-rated on

TripAdvisor. They serve a 10 curry meal for only $10. We went there early as the reviews on TripAdvisor mentioned the place is packed every night. Since we know that most people eat at 8 pm, we decide to go at 6 pm and indeed the place is empty, there's only a couple of people. The curries were good, but cold as usual. Really nothing special, but at $10 with enough food for two people it is definitely the cheapest place to eat in the Fort.

After dinner we decide to go walk around the Fort, we're running low on money and we don't know if the ATM machines are going to work. There are two or three banks in the Fort so we decide to go try them. First bank we tried failed. Second bank failed. We're not so hopeful of the third bank and indeed it fails as well. We've been trying our debit cards, but at the last bank I decide to try my MasterCard because we absolutely need more money to eat at these expensive restaurants here. This time it works, we go back to the hotel and I pay my MasterCard right away.

We go to bed early and are really looking forward to leaving this country.

DAY 15: SARAH'S TAKE

Another day, another free breakfast. I've been pretty good at trying most of the meals, but today it's inedible. Hard as it is to mess up eggs, toast and fresh fruit, they manage to ruin all three. I had another dreadful sleep last night and this doesn't help my immune system fight off the cold. Not caring that the milk has an odd chunky texture and that there are bugs crawling through the sugar bowl and teacup, I happily slurp my caffeine.

We head out to visit the fortifications. It's hot and very sunny, so I bring my umbrella to protect me from the sun. I am hot in my sneakers, but I enjoy the walk because it is along the elevated walls and there are no vehicles. I like looking at the architecture and imagining life during the 420+ years since the fort's construction.

Everywhere I go, I enjoy imagining a mental movie of typical day-to-day life. How do people eat, do laundry, go to the store... I like to reflect on it all. It's even more interesting in an historic site because there are many decades to imagine. So far, it has been very difficult to plunge into the fort's history because of all the tuk tuks and cars on the road. A bummer for me because that was one of the main reasons I wanted to stay here. I get a better feel for the history up on these walls.

The ancient relics along the fort wall are unprotected, victim to vandalism, and pretty much crumbling. We see old staircases, turrets, and other unidentified fort constructions. When we finally get to a stretch of wall that looks better preserved, I see a plaque providing some historical information. Information! That's what was oddly missing in many parts of the fort. Cedric tells me there's a museum (admission fee) that explains it in more detail.

Later, when I'm too hot in my sneakers and out of clean socks, we go buy more socks and a cheap pair of sandals. I want to buy simple flip flops, but somehow the salesman convinces me to buy a fancier pair of black strappy sandals. As we walk back, the new shoes are pinching my feet and by the time we get back to the hotel my toes are raw and bleeding.

I change back into my sneakers at the hotel and we head out for an early dinner, 10 curries for 950 rupees. The restaurant is down a narrow alley in the fort. We are seated next to the 6-foot wall separating the alley from the residence and it's beautifully covered with vegetation. The food is OK, not great. Typical salty, bland Sri Lankan curries. Same as we've had most everywhere. However, they have EGB and it's ample food for cheap, so I'm happy.

Until Cedric spots a large rat walking along the wall, right next to my head. Yes, this is a fort; they had rats back in the day, of course they still do. I've seen the gutters here and shouldn't be surprised. But this puts me off the meal and I just pick at the food until we leave.

We spend the rest of the evening strolling the fort and looking for an ATM. The fort is beautifully lit at night, especially the mosque. Just like in Polonnaruwa, we have trouble with the cash machines. There are a slew of other tourists hanging outside the bank, complaining about their cards not working. One of the machines finally works with Cedric's MasterCard.

DAY 16: JANUARY 2, 2015

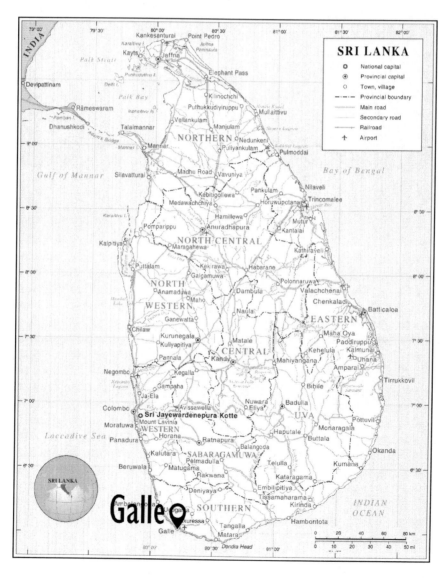

It's 1 am and I'm being woken up by the TV that got turned on. It's quite loud, somebody is watching a movie. I hope it won't last long.

It's 3 am and the TV is finally turned off. I am so tired, I fall back asleep instantly.

It's 7 am and I'm being woken up by how bright the room is in the morning. I am so tired, I only slept a few hours. I am really, really looking forward to leaving this country. This has been a really long and mostly unpleasant trip. This morning we decide to skip the guesthouse's breakfast entirely and go to Crêpe-ology.

We eat a nice breakfast and write on our laptops. When we've had enough, we go back to the hotel to drop off our stuff. Finally, there is no one in the common area, right outside our room. So we write here for a while until the family comes back and the little boy turns on the TV to max volume. I am extremely happy at the thought of leaving the city tomorrow. We'll be taking the train to Colombo and it should be a relatively comfortable ride.

For dinner, we head back to Rocket Burger and it's really tasty again. Just pricey for such small burgers.

We go to bed early once again...at least we try. The TV is quite loud. Since we cannot sleep because of the noise, it's a good opportunity to work on this book. Tomorrow we are leaving for Colombo. Have I mentioned that I am absolutely looking forward to it? This hotel is so bad, it can only get better. Finally at 11 pm, the TV is turned off and I fall asleep immediately.

DAY 16: SARAH'S TAKE

After another dreadful sleep due to some late night TV watching, I wake up to the resident kids and family at around 6:30 or 7 am. Of course our "room" is right next to the kitchen and they are working hard to ruin breakfast for the other patrons. (Sorry, grouchy this morning.) We head to our crêpe restaurant for breakfast. I order a jug of iced tea (so that we can sip it and linger) and the huevos rancheros crêpe. Absolutely delicious; the scrambled eggs are perfectly light and fluffy, yet dense and creamy. All I can say is wow. The crêpe batter has some fresh herbs in the mix. Topped with tasty salsa and guacamole served with an awesome potato salad. Cedric orders a sweet crêpe with chocolate hazelnut and fresh pineapples. We work and write at the restaurant, but after 4 hours here, I want to leave. Cedric successfully pays with his credit card. I guess it depends on the restaurant.

We come back to the hotel and the family is not in living room, so we decide to occupy this space and continue to write. The A/C is supposed to be fixed, but it's still not working. I leave our room door open with the fan on to try airing it out. The family returns and the air conditioner repair man arrives at around the same time. We wait for him to fix the A/C. Yay! We might sleep better tonight.

We decide on spicy chicken burgers at the burger joint for supper. We sit out on the second floor balcony to enjoy our meal. It's a nice view of the street and setting sun.

We stroll around the fort after supper, gaze out at the ocean and then head back to the hotel for an early night. Of course, the TV doesn't allow that. Normally, I don't like to waste electricity because I know these Sri Lankan guesthouse owners are not wealthy, but I blast the A/C all night, hoping it will drown out the TV and we can get some sleep.

DAY 17: JANUARY 3, 2015

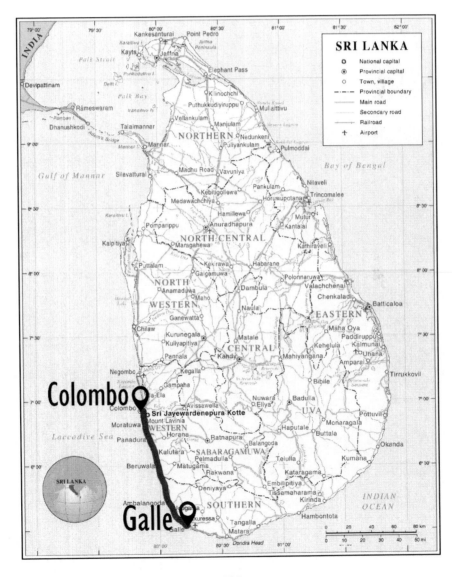

Today we are leaving! These three days in Galle felt like forever. The train is at 4:30 pm, so we go eat one last time at Crêpe-ology before taking the train for Colombo. We spend most of the day there, just waiting for our train time.

The train station is really close, only a 10-minute walk. Since we already have our tickets, we can go in right away. But before we do, some salesperson is harassing us, asking us if we want to buy tickets. I tell him we already have our tickets, but he doesn't seem bothered, still continuing his speech about how his tickets are cheaper than at the ticket office. Again, I tell him we already have tickets, but he doesn't care. He persists with his speech that we should buy tickets from him. He is so persistent and he is walking with us, in front of us, blocking our way. We must buy tickets from him, he insists. This guy doesn't want to hear a word that I'm saying. I keep telling him we already have tickets, but he doesn't care. So I reach for Sarah's backpack and take the tickets out. As soon as he sees the tickets, he leaves immediately, just as quickly as he rushed towards us to sell us his tickets. We were so eager to leave this city that we got to the train station an hour early. It's not very crowded, so we wait patiently on the deck.

When the train finally arrives, we are clueless as to which cart to board. The carts are not identified. I see what looks like an employee about 200 meters farther away on the deck. I show him my ticket, and he says we are in the

136

first cart (right next to where we were in the first place). We walked to the first cart and get in. Much to our surprise, our 2nd class seats are a private cabin with a curtain. There is even a power outlet and a little table in front of our seats. We are able to plug in our tablet and watch some videos. This is quite the contrast from any other mode of transportation that we've taken so far in this country. After being in the worst hotel for the past three days, this is the best surprise in a long time. It feels amazing.

The train ride is so nice. We are moving along the west coast of the country and the tracks are really close to the water. Somehow we lucked into seats with a view of the ocean side, so we have a magnificent view most of the way. As we are near our destination, I notice on Google maps that there is a train station really close to our hotel, but I have no idea if the train will stop at that train station. So far, the train has stopped at every single train station along the way, but in this country I've learnt to never expect anything. Just in case the train stops, Sarah and I grab our bags and head to the front of our cart. I am looking on Google maps, but it's not very precise. After 5 to 10 minutes of waiting at the front of the cart, I'm pretty sure we passed our train station. Seems like the train did not stop. But it's okay, we'll just have to take a tuk tuk to our hotel. A few minutes later we arrive at Colombo Fort train station. For the first time in our trip, we are in a place we've been before. This is where it all started; this is where we arrived from Negombo (our first guesthouse) and took the train to Anuradhapura. It feels good to be in familiar territory.

We exit the train and make our way out of the train station. It doesn't take more than 10 seconds before a tuk tuk driver approaches us. We tell him the name of our hotel and he knows right away where it is. He says, "Let's go, I can take you there."

I asked him, "How much?"

He says, "500 rupees."

I wave my hand and tell him, "Forget it, it's way too much," and walk away.

Immediately, he tells me, "Okay, 400 rupees."

I say, "Okay let's go."

Let me tell you one important lesson I've learned in this country. The art of negotiating. The way to negotiate is basically... well... to not negotiate. The only times I was able to successfully negotiate the price down is that as soon as they tell me the price, I wave them off with my hand, tell them to forget it because it's way too much, and walk away. This is the only way they will lower the price. If you actually try to negotiate, by doing a price battle, it will rarely work; they won't budge, at least not in my experience.

As we arrived to our hotel, we are surprised by how good it looks. It's a hostel, but we booked a private room. The common area looks really nice, there are big couches and a TV. Our room is small, but looks really comfy and we have a TV. Best of all, it's really private. It feels so good to be in a comfy, private room that we just lie in bed for a couple of hours and relax. It's like a huge weight has lifted off my shoulders. It feels like I'm breathing for the first time in weeks. We're starting to get really hungry and I can see on Google maps that there is a mall close by. We decide to just walk there, it's only a 5-minute walk.

The mall is pretty good, there is a Food City (grocery store), KFC, Pizza Hut and other small restaurants. There is also lots of shops and even a movie theatre. I was wondering if this country had any movie theatres at all. Now I have my answer. This mall is actually better than the alleged state-of-the-art mall in Kandy. We have a few choices for eating. We are really hesitating between KFC and Pizza Hut. After realising that KFC was probably going to give our stomach a hard time, we head to Pizza Hut.

Their menu is really awesome. It's really adapted to the Sri Lankan culture. Half of the menu is composed of Indian and Sri Lankan inspired meals pizzas. This is really exciting as we love to try new foods, and most importantly we absolutely love Indian food. So the idea of an Indian pizza is really exciting. We decide to order a medium sized Tandoori Chicken pizza which comes with breadsticks for just over $10. A really good deal.

The pizza turns out to be absolutely delicious. We are already excited to come back and try the other Indian pizza options. Surprisingly, 30 minutes after our meal our stomach is not upset. Normally, every time I have fast food, my stomach gets really upset.

After our meal, we go to Food City and buy some water and chocolate and snacks. We go back to our hotel, relax, and breathe. Did I say relax? We've now been in this country for three weeks. It has been a very tiring trip, to say the least. We are glad we did it, but we are also glad it's over. Tomorrow will be our last full day here. Good night.

DAY 17: SARAH'S TAKE

Get me out of here! Our train isn't until the afternoon and the thought of spending all day here is depressing. Instead of the hotel's complimentary breakfast, I just order a pot of free coffee. We wait around at the hotel until we are good and hungry. Then we pack up our bags and bring them to the crêpe restaurant. We eat leisurely, knowing that we have the entire day to burn. Again, it's delicious. After about as much time as is decent for one meal, we leave and spend some time near the beach. There are quite a few Muslim families at the beach, the children are playing in the ocean. Unfortunately, there is a huge collection of garbage near the beach (washed up or deposited), so we don't venture over there. We head to the train station early and I have the pleasure of experiencing a squat toilet in the train station.

We take the train into Colombo and it's a great ride. I'm sure if we would have been able to take the train for the rest of the trip, it would have been great. We are traveling along the ocean and see some amazing scenery. We pass through towns and little communities living on the beach.

The sun is setting as we near Colombo and there starts to be more tourist, resort-type places on the beach. These look wonderful and I wonder how much they cost per night.

Arriving at the now familiar Colombo train station, Cedric negotiates a tuk tuk to our hostel. On the ride, we pass a large beach in town. Even though dusk approaches, it's full of people, food stalls and seems very lively.

I'm impressed by the Clock Inn Colombo; it's really clean and nicely decorated, not like any hostel I've ever stayed. It's more like a hotel. After relaxing in our room for a while, we head out to the mall for something to eat. Our hotel is on Galle Road, which seem to be a main boulevard. The mall is perfect. There is a grocery store on the main level and a food court in the basement. It's kind of late and the food court is mostly closed. We head to the main floor for KFC. We actually walk into the restaurant, but then I see piles of fried chicken sitting out under heat lamps and notice the menu prices are quite high. Through the window of KFC, we see a Pizza Hut and decide to go there instead. Boy, are we glad we did. They had some Indian menu items and our pizza was spicy, cheesy and flavourful.

I love when American chains adapt their menu for the culture. Probably because I grew up with the Ham & Pineapple classic, I like the idea of something new. We've read that India has a lot of adapted menus: McDonalds, Subway, etc. They all have vegetarian dishes and extra menu items. We have always been intrigued by this and love Indian food as well.

I'm happy to be able to try it out here in Sri Lanka. Because after visiting what some call "India Light" (Sri Lanka as a toned down version of India), it will be years before we are ready for India. I'm thinking we would want to budget for nicer hotels and nicer restaurants.

We go to bed full, comfortable and eager to be almost home.

DAY 18: JANUARY 4, 2015

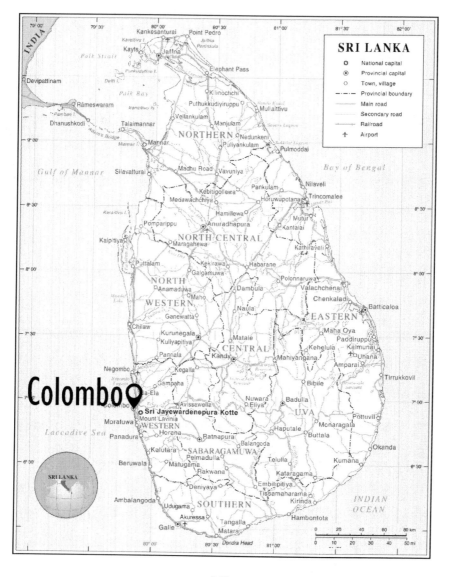

Once again, breakfast is included in our hotel rate. We are used to below average breakfasts, so we are not expecting much. We go downstairs to the common area where breakfast is served. There are a few cooks behind the counter cooking omelettes. It seems like they are cooking fresh omelettes. Very impressive. One of the cook asks us if we want an omelette to which we immediately replied yes. There is also another counter with your typical continental breakfast items. The good thing is you get to toast your own bread yourself, at least this time you know the toast will be fresh. I put two slices of bread in the toaster and by the time they are ready my omelette is also ready. The omelette is a delight, easily the best omelette we've had in this country. It is steaming hot and absolutely delicious. This hotel is turning out to be one of the best hotel we stayed at in this country.

Today we don't have much planned. We just want to relax before our long travel day tomorrow. For lunch we decide to go back to our new favourite restaurant, Pizza Hut. This time trying their Moghul Chicken Tandoori Pizza. Again, delicious.

On the way there, there is a huge screen broadcasting messages from the President for the electoral campaign. The screen is located on the building of the electoral office of the President. People gather on the street and watch it. As it is in Sinhalese, I don't understand a word of it. JP's comments on the President and all this electoral activity makes me more and more curious about the whole thing. I decide to go online and read news articles about the election.

From what I am reading, the President is evidently highly corrupt. He is running against other candidates who, in most part, don't stand a chance. However, there is one candidate who stands a chance. He is an old advisor of the President who stepped down and decided to run in the election himself. He is building his campaign on unity. He wants to end corruption and wants more peace between the Tamil and Sinhalese. That is quite a contrast from the current President who publicly speaks against the Tamils on a daily basis. The current President is way ahead in the polls at around 60% for him and 30% for his contender. So, unfortunately, hopes of dethroning the current President are slim to none. Corruption is a plague in this country. It is obviously one of the main reason why the country hasn't been developing more. Contrary to the United States and other first world countries where corruption is more hidden and done behind closed doors, corruption in Sri Lanka is evident and obvious and simply part of life. Corruption is probably the easiest way to get out of poverty. So most people would not hesitate to corrupt if given the opportunity.

Spending our last day in this country, I am genuinely saddened by the general state of it. I can't wait to leave this country, but for the population living here, most of them will spend their entire life here. I know that humans adapt to everything and that, for them, this life is probably not that hard. But I can't help to feel for them. It's hard to understand how a country like Great Britain and other first world countries can evolve so rapidly, while other countries like Sri Lanka barely evolve at all over hundreds of years. If the British hadn't come 100 years ago to build railways, set up tea plantations and uncover the artifacts that are now considered UNESCO sites and are bringing millions of tourists to the country, then it's hard to dispute that Sri Lanka would definitely be worse off. They are still using the same tracks, the same trains, the same train stations that the British built 100 years ago, and are using it to full capacity. What would this country be like if the British hadn't come and built the railways? Would the Sri Lankans have built it themselves? Allow me to seriously doubt that. Whether you are for or against the colonization of the British, it seems evident to me that the Sri Lankans *today* are better off because the British came. In the short time that they were here, the British pushed the development of this country through the roof. And ever since they left, it's like the country has been put on pause.

Tomorrow we are taking the plane at 6 am. Since we absolutely do not want to miss our flight and the airport is about an hour drive from our hotel, we've booked a 3 am taxi through our hotel for 2,000 rupees. Surprisingly, that's about the same amount it costs for the 15-minute ride from the airport to our hotel at the beginning of our trip.

For dinner, we go to Pizza Hut once again and try another one of their Indian pizzas. It is once again a delight. Since we are getting up at 2:30 am to catch our flight, we go to bed early and try to get as much sleep as possible.

DAY 18: SARAH'S TAKE

Today we can relax. I am very excited for the trip back to Thailand. We got up early to reserve our seats on the plane. Cedric found out that the exit row is the same price as all the other seats. You can't recline or store your things under the seat in this row, but it's tons of legroom. So we reserve our seats at the exit row.

We head down to the common area for breakfast. Firstly, I didn't notice how nice the common area was yesterday when we checked-in. It has a large carpeted area with cushions, then an L-shaped couch and flat screen TV playing a movie, and 5 square, four-person tables. There are cooks preparing your eggs to order at a small stovetop and you serve yourself the rest of your continental breakfast at another counter. Impressive.

We head back to the room and relax again. I take the time to remove some chunks of mud and dirt from my plane outfit. It smells terrible and I think of the poor person who has to endure me on the plane tomorrow. I try steaming out the stink. The bathroom is smaller in this hotel and they supply hangers, so I hang up my plane outfit and turn on the shower's hot water full blast. I let the water run for a couple minutes and shut it off when the bathroom fills up with steam. I keep the door closed for a while, then let my clothes hang there for the rest of the day. Far from smelling fresh, it does make a difference. Since I need a clean pair of socks for tomorrow and we've relaxed enough, we decide to go shopping at our new favourite mall and then head to Pizza Hut for lunch.

As we walk down Galle Road toward the mall, we pass a woman sitting on the sidewalk, leaned up against the building. She has a disfigured leg and is begging for money. After visiting several stores selling socks at 400 rupees, I find a pair at Bata for 200. We head to Pizza Hut and are approached by a woman holding out her hand. She follow us as we walk and concentrates her pleading efforts on Cedric. She does not follow us into the restaurant.

Pizza Hut seats us at the front of the store, next to their windowed storefront. There is also a speaker blasting annoying music. So Cedric and I can't chat much as we eat. Through the glass, I can see the woman begging everyone who passes, following them until they enter a store. Even stepping into a tuk tuk doesn't dissuade her, she continues to plead with them until the tuk tuk drives away.

We head back to the hotel and relax. Before you know it, it's time to eat again. We pass a lot of grubby-looking restaurants serving cheap food. Many cooks prepare food right next to the windowed storefront, so we can watch them from the street. You can hear the rhythmic and distinctive clang of metal-on-metal as they fry/chop kottu roti. It kind of reminds me of a dinner bell. If we had stronger stomachs, I would like to try some of these dishes. Since we have weak North American constitutions, we head to Pizza Hut where things are cooked at 500°F.

The waiter tries to seat us at the window again, but I stop him and insist we sit in the back. Not only is it annoying to be gawked at through the window while we eat (probably why he seats us there, "Look, we have white people in our restaurant!"), it's right next to their booming speaker. We sit in the back and it's much more peaceful. We have another delicious pizza and head back to the hotel for an early night.

DAY 19: JANUARY 5, 2015

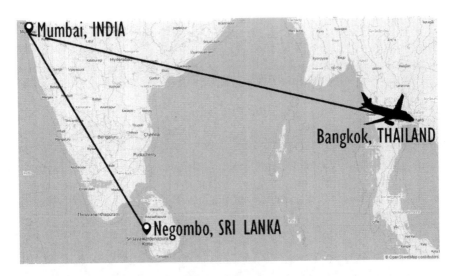

It's 2:30 am and we are getting ready to leave. Today is going to be a long day. We are first taking a flight to Mumbai, where we have a six hour layover, then we take a flight to Bangkok to then take a bus to Hua Hin, our hometown, to arrive at around 10 pm. I can't wait to get back to my version of civilization.

It's 3 am and we go downstairs to find a taxi waiting for us. It is the smallest car I have ever seen in my life. Think the Mini Cooper is small? Think again. You haven't seen a TATA car. It almost looks like a toy car, barely bigger than a tuk tuk. Like toy cars that parents buy for their kids. As we are driving towards the airport, there is an army checkpoint. The taxi stops for a few seconds while two army soldiers point their flashlights at our faces. Seemingly satisfied, they nod to the driver and we are driving again. Once outside Colombo, we are taking the newly built highway that's going to take us directly to the airport. It is a toll highway, costing 300 rupees.

TIP 72 – There is a toll highway between the airport and Colombo. If

you are leaving the country, make sure you allocate some cash for this surprise fee (was 300 rupees in January 2015).

The highway is completely deserted. We are the only car on the highway, driving at around 60 km/h. There is no one in front of us, and almost no one passing us the whole time. I cannot believe that we just paid to take an express highway to only drive at 60 km/h the whole way. It just doesn't seem like we're saving that much time since it's the middle of the night and the regular roads are probably not jammed. Nothing ceases to surprise me in this country. It seems like 60 km/h is about the maximum speed this car can go. I am once again paying first world prices for this less than first world service. On a positive note, I am not afraid for my life. We arrive at the airport safely and take our flight as scheduled.

This marks the end of our adventure, and let me tell you, an adventure it was. I don't regret taking this trip to Sri Lanka, but I am happy it's over. I will forever remember this trip. I would have to say—and I know it's going to sound silly—but the best thing about Sri Lanka that I discovered on this trip is ginger beer. Not just any ginger beer, Elephant House Ginger Beer or "EGB." Coca-Cola has their own version of ginger beer, but it's not nearly as good because it's made from artificial ginger. Elephant House Ginger Beer is absolutely delicious, my new favourite drink. It's a bit spicy and has a very powerful ginger taste. If you're a fan of ginger, you will absolutely love this drink.

DAY 19: SARAH'S TAKE

Could this TATA go any slower? It's still dark and we are headed to the airport. I cannot understand why the taxi driver is going 60 km/h when the speed limit is 100 and the few cars on the road are zooming past us. I ask the driver, "How fast can you go on this road?"

He answers, "30 minutes ma'am." Recognizing that I'm grouchy from a lack of caffeine and sleep, I don't press the issue. I'm so eager to leave that it's making me impatient, more so than usual, and I'm an impatient person. I do not want to spend another day in this country and cannot miss our plane.

TIP 73 – When you are headed to the airport from Colombo, ask for a taxi that can go 100 km/h on the toll highway. But don't expect to get this and just leave earlier for the airport.

The airport looks the same. It was dark and raining when we arrived, it's exactly the same as we are leaving. We head inside and pass a security scan. Our bags are run through a machine and I am handed off to a female security agent for a feeble pat down. That's the extent of the security check; it takes about 15 seconds. The airline counters are empty, we get checked-in in about 5 minutes. Then we head over to Immigration to officially exit the country. Here we are held up for a good 30 minutes. Not sure what is so complicated about checking a person out of the country, but it seems to take an eternity to pass each person. We finally get through and walk to the terminal.

We pass the currency exchange area and I tell Cedric that we should exchange our rupees. He says we can just wait until Thailand because we might need the cash. Very unusual for me, I insist. All the exchange counters are ghost towns except one, which is extremely busy. We visit one of the dead ones. I ask if they have Thai baht and she says no, only USD. I tell her how much I have and she gives me a number. It seems quite low compared to what Google says we should get, so I ask her to explain it. Basically, their rate just sucks and their commission fee is ridiculously high. I decide to get another quote. We wait in line behind the busy counter and get a much better offer. Of course, there is usually a reason why a place is busy.

TIP 74 – At the airport, (or anywhere) get a couple of quotes from different exchange booths. Tell them verbally how much you have

because if you give them the money, they might just start the exchange process.

We sit and wait around for our boarding time. We have lots of unused minutes in our Dialog plan, so Cedric and I phone back home. As we wait out the clock, I resist the urge to buy a coffee, knowing it will be free on the plane. From where we are seated, I see numerous families where the women wear full, patterned skirts with matching full, cape-like, long-sleeved blouses and bonnets. It's Little House on the Prairie (cloth patterns) meets the Hutterites. The women are each herding at least four young children. I like their lively outfits, but can't believe how much the parents (let's face it: the men) must be spending to fly with all these little kids.

We board the plane and experience luxurious legroom. We stretch out and it's so comfortable. The guy behind me keeps hitting the back of my seat, but on our next plane we are in the exit row in front of this one, so that no one will be able to reach the seat. I eat a mediocre breakfast omelette, chicken sausage round, sautéed potatoes, bun and butter and coffee.

TIP 75 – Reserve your flight with Jet Airways if you can. Free alcohol, loads of food and no additional charge for sitting at the exit row. If there are two consecutive exit rows, pick the front because no one will bump into your seat.

At the Mumbai airport, we eagerly wait for our favourite Punjab Grill to stop serving breakfast. I'm sure they would have something amazing, but I don't know what to order. We wait for the butter chicken to be ready and it takes forever because they are making the naan…fresh, so damn fresh. I enjoy it with masala chai.

Then we buy some duty-free vodka. It was only $30 USD for two bottles. It was kind of a silly purchase because neither of us likes vodka. Juice (mixer) isn't even cheap in Thailand. I guess it's just a lingering teenager mentality where you have to buy the cheapest thing with the highest alcohol content. Next time, we will accept our age and buy some nice wine, which is really expensive in Thailand anyway.

When it's finally time to board, we are waiting at the gate. They do something I've never experienced, they don't call any particular rows. I always thought the calling of rows was a thing airline companies did to allow 1st classers to feel superior. Turns out it's got a practical purpose too. Because everyone is boarding at once, the line is incredibly slow moving and everyone is jamming up the aisles to let people get seated and installed beside them. No one seems to be able to find any more room in the overhead bins. It's an absolute gong show.

To make it worse, after everything seems settled, the flight crew is moving people around in the seats. "Oh, this woman has a baby. Let's move her up front. Is the guy up front okay with the woman being moved beside him? No. Let's move you back here then, sir. And be sure to move your bags around too." They are moving so many people around in their designated seats that what was the point even assigning them in the first place? Despite perfect weather, we leave 1 hour late because of the poorly organized nonsense.

Ah, but the seats are worth it. Cedric and I are pleased as punch about the extra legroom. It is truly outstanding. I take the snack (spicy mango powder fried dal) with a free beer (Tiger brand from Singapore). The meal is good. They only have vegetarian options left, curried vegetable, rice, paneer with green sauce, roti. I'm incredibly full, but can't get enough of all this free food.

When we arrive at the Bangkok airport, I ask a currency exchange booth if they take Sri Lanka Rupee. The normally stone-faced agent has a good, long laugh then looks at me with pity and shakes her head no. Thank goodness I didn't listen to Cedric on this one.

BONUS TIP – Exchange all LKR to USD or EUR before you leave the country. Sri Lankan Rupees aren't a hot commodity in the world and you'll be hard pressed to find a currency exchange interested in buying them from you.

Arriving so late in Bangkok really messes up our plans. We miss the last bus back to Hua Hin and entrust our lives to an overtired taxi driver who takes mini naps at the wheel while driving at 110 km/h (yikes!). I started my day in Sri Lanka, stressed about a taxi driver who was going too slow. I finished my day in Thailand, stressed about a taxi driver who was going too fast.

AFTERWORD

We've been back in Thailand for a few weeks. Since our diet consisted mainly of starches (rice, bread, lentils) and we were trying not to drink too much water for the long bus/train/taxi rides, I stopped pooping at around Day 10. Constipated for 14 days, I had to visit the hospital in Thailand for some help back there. Make sure to drink plenty of water during your trip!

Looking back on this trip, I have to say I'm really glad I did it. I've learned so much about myself, the world, and most importantly I've learned to appreciate what I have in life. I watched the news today and saw that Sri Lanka's President was defeated by his number one contender. I must say I am extremely surprised by that fact. All the newspapers gave the current President a win. I also read that the defeated President tried to keep power by force when he learned of his defeat, but that the army refused to follow his orders. This is very good news for this country. It probably won't be a revolution, but I believe it's a step in the right direction.

If you are considering a trip to Sri Lanka (which I assume you are if you are reading this book), and only have 2 or 3 weeks of holidays, I recommend skipping the north entirely, or at least spending less time there. The areas we actually enjoyed the most by far are Kandy, Nuwara Eliya and Ella.

Looking back, I would have spent a lot more time in these three cities, especially Kandy, and less time in the north and south, especially the north. Kandy is absolutely gorgeous, set in a small plain amongst the jungle mountains, it is the highlight of the country in my opinion. We stayed at Hanthana Holiday Rooms, I highly recommend this guesthouse, the food is delicious, it's clean and the family is very welcoming.

Nuwara Eliya is worth it just for Loga's food (Nidwalden Resort), some of the best food I've eaten in my life, but make sure to bring a jacket as it can get cold there. The local population wear winter jackets! Many shops sell winter apparel there if you don't have any. This city is also home to a lot of tea plantations that you can visit. Make sure to go to Nuwara Eliya and/or Ella by train, but reserve in advance online through one of the two private train companies (Rajadhani Express or Expo Rail). It's inexpensive and tickets sell out fast, so make sure to reserve as much in advance as you can.

In Ella, make sure to book a hotel with a view. We stayed at the Green Hill Guest House Ella and while the food was average, the room was good and the view was spectacular. Make sure to reserve as much in advance as possible as these guesthouses only have a few rooms so they sell out fast.

You will be rewarded with breathtaking views that are simply priceless.

Another plus of not going in the north is you'll be able to avoid uncomfortable bus rides as there are no train tracks to the major UNESCO sites in the north. If you stick to the middle and south of the country, you'll be able to take the much more comfortable train rides (provided you reserve in advance and there are no landslides). Most of the major cities in the middle and south of the country are reachable by train.

We didn't spend that much time in Colombo and regret it a little bit. You might want to consider spending a few nights there. In general, the activities that we enjoyed the most in Sri Lanka were the ones that didn't cost much money. The most interesting experiences that we will actually remember for a long time were just walking in the cities/towns and observing the local life and/or the magnificent view, eating delicious foods, or talking with our hosts and learning so much about Sri Lankan culture.

Sri Lankan people are very poor, and unfortunately it's rare to encounter someone whose sole intention is not to get as much money from you as possible, whether it's a tuk tuk driver, a person begging or someone selling something. You rarely get a free hello, there is always an intention behind every interaction. They are very persistent and don't give up easily. We noticed that the vast majority of tuk tuk drivers (there are exceptions) have a very bad attitude and seem to hate their job (despite charging you around 10 times what they would charge a local for the same service). It would be the equivalent of charging 500 euros to tourists for a short taxi journey in Europe, you'd think the drivers would be happy. This is a mystery I have yet to solve. My suspicion is that there is some sort of tuk tuk mafia operating and the drivers have to distribute most of their profit to the mafia if they want to operate their taxis. I know it seems far-fetched but it's the only thing I can think of that makes sense.

We found that the nicest people were in Nuwara Eliya and Ella. It's the only place in the country where we got some genuine, free hellos. The tea picking ladies were particularly nice and some of the few people we saw smile and say hello without asking for money.

AFTERWORD: SARAH'S TAKE

There are three Sri Lankan things that I often long to re-experience: EGB (Elephant House Ginger Beer), Loga's food at the Nidwalden Resort in Nuwara Eliya, and the view from our Ella guesthouse. There are a number of Sri Lankan things that I would rather not re-experience and, lucky for me, I won't have to.

After we left Sri Lanka, we came back to the same town in Thailand and somehow I saw everything differently. Without intention or any deliberation, I felt gratitude. Sri Lanka has marked me for life.

I can reassure you that it is a safe place to visit. Note that we have felt unsafe during many of our trips to the United States, if that provides any comparison. I would recommend Sri Lanka to anyone looking for an interesting holiday and who is physically able to handle it (this is not a country that can easily accommodate physical disability).

My only regret is not buying some spices to take home. Galle is very touristy and many places sold food souvenirs, like Sri Lankan tea and spices. There was the famous "true cinnamon" (Ceylon cinnamon), but I wish I had bought some asafoetida and mango powder to turn my ordinary curries into extraordinary. I didn't buy any because I assumed Thailand would have these ingredients, but I was wrong.

TIPS RECAP

1. This is a cash country. If you prefer to bring cash (vs. using Sri Lankan ATM), bring USD or EUR. You will get a better rate than your home currency and it will be more easily exchanged.
2. Make sure you have your guesthouse phone number for your taxi driver. Unless you are staying in a major hotel (and even then), chances are he will need to call them for directions.
3. If you will be staying in 2 -3 stars guesthouses, bring soap as most of them don't provide any (or they will provide used bars of soap if any). Bring bar soap if the plane won't let you travel with liquid.
4. Bring USD, EUR or credit card to pay for food etc. in your layover airport.
5. Bring a pen in your carry on to fill out your arrival card on the plane or in the airport where either there will be no pen or 10 people will be waiting to use it.
6. Unless you are from Singapore, Seychelles or the Maldives (you don't need a visa if you are from one of these countries), buy your visa online (http://www.eta.gov.lk/slvisa/) prior to arriving. It's a bit cheaper than getting a visa on arrival, the process is very easy and efficient and it will be one less thing to worry about when arriving in Sri Lanka.
7. If you will be using a debit card for ATM withdrawals, make sure it's got the Cirrus, Plus or Maestro logo on the back. But as you will find out later in this book, even if your card and the ATM machine have one of the corresponding major logos, the transaction might still fail, especially in small towns. For this reason, bring a zero balance credit card exclusively for ATM cash advances, just in case your debit card doesn't work. Don't forget to bring your online banking info to pay it back right away. However, even credit cards might still not work either in smaller towns. You best bet is to withdraw money in one of the two major cities in the country, namely Colombo (metropolitan) and Kandy. If you need to withdraw money at the airport, there are a couple of ATMs near the exit, not too far from the taxi counters. They worked for us.
8. Make sure to bring an unlocked phone, get your free SIM card from Dialog at the airport and just follow the instructions to activate it, it's actually very easy. Once the SIM card is activated, you need to buy a plan. Get the tourist plan. To buy it (if the guy at the Dialog counter in the airport doesn't want to do it), you can go to any shop in the city with the big Dialog logo. We went to a shop near the Colombo Fort

train station, it was very easy and they were very helpful. Also, Sri Lanka has a different GSM cellular frequency than North America. Make sure your cell phone can handle the 900/1800 bands.

9. Get the taxi to write down the price if there is the slightest hint of miscommunication.

10. Change out of your warm plane clothes before leaving the airport. Many taxis have no air conditioning.

11. Contact your host beforehand to determine the reasonable taxi fare from the airport to their accommodation.

12. Most guesthouses will offer complimentary tea when you arrive and it's rather impolite to refuse it.

13. Kind Sri Lankan exception: most tuk tuk drivers will bend the truth in their favour. If you need to ask them something, make sure you corroborate their information with other people.

14. Forget about saving a couple bucks with the train's 3rd class, get your reserved 1st or 2nd class seats if they are available. Also, determine if your travel dates include Sri Lankan school or national holidays. If so, more locals will be filling up trains and buses throughout the country. Things may be fully booked and packed with people. In that case, definitely book your train tickets in advance through an agent online.

15. Ask your host plenty of questions. Input with a local perspective is invaluable.

16. The train is a must and seats can sell out quickly. When we travelled, Sri Lanka Railways train tickets could be reserved 45 days in advance, but not online. You must be in Sri Lanka to buy these tickets. You can book online with private train carriages (ExpoRail, Rajadhani) or contact your hotel/local travel agencies to secure them on your behalf. Consider the most scenic side of the train carriage (west side if travelling Galle to Colombo for ocean view) and select these seats.

17. Take into account that the train's reservation offices close for lunch between noon and 1 pm.

18. There are 2 types of power outlets that are equally used. To plug in your electronics, get the universal adapter or just buy both adapter types because they only cost a couple dollars in Sri Lanka (compared to $30 at the Mumbai airport).

19. After the cell phone store sets up your cell plan, make sure you try calling/browsing the web before you leave the store. They may have to do additional tweaking on your foreign phone.

20. Some stores and restaurants that accept credit cards may actually block foreign cards, so be sure to have some cash on hand.

21. You can jump off to pee or get something to eat during train/bus canteen breaks. Just hurry up and remember which carriage is yours!

22. The risk for malaria is indeed present in the north of the country, but it

is still a very, very small risk, almost nonexistent, probably less than a fraction of a fraction of a percent. Malaria is transmitted by a type of mosquito that bites at night, particularly in deep forested area (i.e. on a train passing through jungles). Antimalarial drugs are usually not recommended as the risk is too low. The general recommendation is to apply DEET to prevent mosquito bites, particularly if you are in a rural area, in the north of the country. This is merely an opinion and not an official recommendation, you should consult a doctor and/or do your own research.

23. If you come across a tuk tuk driver you like, ask for his number for future use in the city.

24. If you plan on eating at the hotel, ask what time they serve meals. Some have quite restricted times.

25. The Anuradhapura ruins are very peaceful and pleasant. Rent a bicycle to tour them if it's not raining. Your guesthouse will be able to arrange anything you need, whether you want to rent bicycles or hire a tuk tuk or even a car. They make a commission from the sales of these services, it's a very big business in small towns like Anuradhapura. If you're on a budget, always try to negotiate.

26. Unless you are in a bigger city, eating at the guesthouse will be your best option. They usually make decent to excellent food that's also inexpensive.

27. The essential oil repellents available in Sri Lanka don't work. Bring DEET from home. Many companies make wipes/towelettes if you your flight has a liquid ban.

28. When visiting Buddhist sites, they ask that you don't wear dark clothing (disrespectful), shoes or hats. So bring a bag to carry your hat and shoes if you will be biking. Light shoes (flip flops) are better since they are lighter to carry and easier to slip on and off.

29. Stock up on water and nuts or dal/mung bean snack at the grocery store because supper at the guesthouse is often served after 8 or 9 pm. Depending on where you are from you may be used to eating at this time (or not).

30. Vegetarians/vegans will be able to respect their diet while travelling in Sri Lanka. Vegetable curries, roti, hoppers and dal (lentil) are staple foods. Just advise your host of your restrictions if you will be eating at the guesthouse.

31. Even in small towns, never feel like there is only one tuk tuk offer on the table. Your best bet is to get a couple of quotes, from different drivers and your guesthouse owner. Sometimes the tuk tuk driver will offer a better price than your guesthouse and vice versa.

32. No matter what it is (restaurant, tuk tuk, souvenir) always ask "How much?" beforehand. Every time we forget to do this, the bill is

staggering.

33. If you want a seat on the bus, you need to embark at the start of the route and get there early.

34. If you visit during a rainy season, consider that these large, high buses are the only vehicle that can drive through deep water. A private car or smaller air conditioned bus aren't high enough off the ground.

35. Ladies, always have toilet paper/tissues in your pocket. Handwashing stations are no guarantee either, so bring hand sanitizer. If the plane won't let you travel with liquid, bring sanitizing wipes.

36. Try the Elephant House Ginger Beer (EGB) as early in your trip as possible. Delicious and soothing for the digestive system, they sell it most places.

37. Unravel and set up the mosquito net over the bed when you arrive at the hotel. Not only does this air them out (often quite musty), but if you wait until night when the mosquitoes are out, you may trap some inside with you.

38. Consider bringing a paper copy of your reservations. While Agoda and other online booking sites claim that you can present an electronic copy of your booking confirmation, we found this doesn't work out at some guesthouses.

39. There are a lot of fake TripAdvisor reviews in Sri Lanka, so take the rave reviews with a grain of salt. A couple places we visited openly offered you discounted or free things to give them a review on the website.

40. Bathroom talk: At the hotels, you generally aren't given toilet paper or a garbage bag in the bathroom. Since you usually don't flush paper, we always keep our plastic grocery bags to use in the bathroom.

41. At the Dambulla Rock Temple, don't take off your shoes at the base of the mountain. Wear them for the climb, your feet will thank you. The sacred space is only a very small fenced area at the top of the mountain.

42. Depending on your appetite, start with one dish and split it (at both restaurants and guesthouses). We found it was always very large portions.

43. Bathroom talk: Ladies, most of the online advice about using a "bum gun" is for men. Usually, the bidet sprayer has the best angle between the legs, from the front.

44. Golden rule: stay away from the buffet. Outrageously expensive, usually not very good, and cold. Depending on your appetite, you will rarely eat enough to make it worth your while.

45. When travelling to Kandy from the north by bus, get off at the Temple of the Tooth. Since it is right before Kandy's ridiculously congested city centre, it will be faster to walk from the Temple than to wait until you arrive at the bus terminal.

46. If you have anything to buy (clothes, food, equipment) or require any service (bank, cell plan) make sure you take care of it in the bigger cities (Colombo, Kandy). Once you get more into the country, you lose options.

47. Curry leaves are edible, but most people push them to the side of their plate. I (Sarah) like to take a small mouthful of food, pick up a leaf, bite down (still intact) to release the amazing aroma, and then push the leaf to the side of my plate. There is no substitute for fresh curry leaves and unless you know someone who is growing a curry tree in in their backyard, this is the only part of the world where you can enjoy the unique aroma.

48. Forget the A/C bus. If it is busy, you will be so squished that you won't feel any A/C, only body heat. Because it's a smaller vehicle, you feel more road bumps too.

49. Don't be shy to ask for more blankets if you need them. The hosts usually have plenty of extra.

50. Eating the Sri Lankan way:
    i.   Wash your hands
    ii. Use your right hand only (one hand will feel awkward, especially tearing bread)
    iii. Tear bread or grab a chunk of rice
    iv. Mix up your rice/curry/sambal/etc.
    v.   Pinch food with your fingertips (if you are using bread, cover food with bread and pinch a little food inside)

    Supposedly, you shouldn't get sauce up higher than your first joint, so really use the tips of your fingers.

51. Definitely walk everywhere in Nuwara Eliya, if you can. It's a small town and you miss much of the charm if you drive around.

52. Flowering season in Nuwara Eliya is April to May and August to September. Victoria Park will be most beautiful around these times.

53. You can opt to hire a private driver for your trip. Although you miss out on a huge part of the Sri Lankan experience by doing this, it is massively more comfortable than the buses, trains and tuk tuks that the masses use. For me (Sarah), my hesitation is not that we would have to pay for all the driver's food and accommodations, it's that they would be with us all the time. Sharing my holidays with a stranger would drive me absolutely mental.

54. If you are chatting with tourists that have already gone to your upcoming destinations, get their opinion on activities, restaurants, etc. in that town. As they are some of the few people in the country not trying to relieve you of your money, their opinion is truly valuable.

55. The Nidwalden Resort in Nuwara Eliya is also a restaurant. So if you booked elsewhere, definitely call to see if you can eat a meal there.

Loga's home cooked food is worth it.

56. If you can't get a seat on the bus to and from Nuwara Eliya, the taxi is worth it because the roads are very curvy and it's a tough ride to do standing.

57. Absolutely consider using the Agoda app. I (Cedric) booked all of our guesthouses through Agoda.com and with their Android application, you see the exact GPS position of each hotel on the map, which came in absolutely essential during this trip because if you simply look for the hotel on Google maps, it's not precise at all. Addresses and street names are not exactly obvious in Sri Lanka, so the Agoda app has been extremely useful.

58. Eat at AK Ristoro for all your non-guesthouse meals in Ella. Otherwise, you are missing out on one of the best restaurants in Sri Lanka.

59. There is usually an employed station agent somewhere in the bus terminal building. He will give you the most accurate bus time and number information. If he feels like it.

60. Make sure your Ella guesthouse has an outstanding view. It's an experience beyond compare and not much difference in price.

61. In Ella, head to Little Adam's Peak early morning before the clouds roll in. Let your host know the night before what your plans are and see if they can have breakfast ready early.

62. Definitely visit Little Adam's Peak. If you can't do steep climbs, just walk until the base of the Peak. The tea planation that you walk through is just as interesting, if not more, than the Peak itself.

63. Bring some water or buy a bottle from one of the little kiosks on your Little Adam's Peak walk. Climbing the Peak itself is a workout.

64. If you want to take a taxi, be sure to ask other travellers at the hotel and at the bus stop if they are going to the same place and split the fare.

65. Though we suspect that these Sri Lankan curry meals are just reheated dishes, they often take 60 to 90 minutes to reach your table. Something to consider before ordering it from the menu.

66. The advantage of hiring a taxi driver between destinations is that you can make stops along the way or go buy some supplies at a store. Don't forget to take advantage of that.

67. It seems like no matter what time you arrive, the room is never ready. Expect to wait around 30 to 60 minutes before you can access the room. If you have somewhere to go, you can usually leave your bags with the host.

68. Always take photos, even when you're hesitant (religious sites). Perhaps momentarily unpleasant, later you will be glad you have the picture.

69. If you go on the Yala National Park safari, consider wearing darker colours and shower thoroughly afterward. Open jeep plus red dirt

roads equals filthy.

70. Many tuk tuk drivers are slow to pick you up from the guesthouse when called. Plan for that tardiness.

71. Galle is interesting but small, so don't plan for more than 2 days in the fort or else you may get bored.

72. There is a toll highway between the airport and Colombo. If you are leaving the country, make sure you allocate some cash for this surprise fee (was 300 rupees in January 2015).

73. When you are headed to the airport from Colombo, ask for a taxi that can go 100 km/h on the toll highway. But don't expect to get this and just leave earlier for the airport.

74. At the airport, (or anywhere) get a couple of quotes from different exchange booths. Tell them verbally how much you have because if you give them the money, they might just start the exchange process.

75. Reserve your flight with Jet Airways if you can. Free alcohol, loads of food and no additional charge for sitting at the exit row. If there are two consecutive exit rows, pick the front because no one will bump into your seat.

BONUS TIP – Exchange all LKR to USD or EUR before you leave the country. Sri Lankan Rupees aren't a hot commodity in the world and you'll be hard pressed to find a currency exchange interested in buying them from you.

NOTES

All of the businesses mentioned in this book are solely for advice purposes and reflect only our personal experience with them. We received absolutely no compensation from any businesses or persons during our trip in Sri Lanka. That includes any restaurant or attraction that we visited. Anything mentioned in this book reflects only our opinion. Any and all businesses mentioned are only for advice in the hope that your trip will be made safer, easier, better, more organised and to avoid some mistakes that we made. We received no compensation whatsoever for mentioning any business or person in this book. We truly think and hope that reading this book will greatly benefit planning your trip in Sri Lanka.

Map data from OpenStreetMap.org available under Open Database License and cartography is licensed as CC BY-SA.

14638627R00094

Printed in Great Britain
by Amazon.co.uk, Ltd.,
Marston Gate.